Living in
Joyful Resilience

A Roadmap for Navigating Life's Ups and Downs

Kate Olson

For a copyright license, visit http://www.copyrightsnow.net/ or call toll free
to copysupport@digi-rights.com
Cataloged in publication information is available from Library and Archives U.S.

ISBN: 978-1-956257-17-5
Formatting, publishing, cover design by Pierucci Publishing

Interior design by Sophie Hanks
Edited by Rachie Bluebell
Cover design by Lisa Robinson, Moon Cat Studio

Dedications

I am happy to dedicate this book to my amazing son, Chris Lemke, my niece, Cieara Erikson and my nephew, James Moleston. They know they are all my favorites! They are all still creating their futures and I hope that they can incorporate more joy into their lives much sooner than I did. I lovingly wish them & their families a future filled with joyful resilience!

Disclaimer

The suggestions and strategies found in this book may not be right for every situation or reader. This work is sold with the understanding that neither the author nor the publisher are held responsible for the results of any advice given in this book. This is a work of nonfiction. No names have been changed, no characters invented and no events fabricated.

Acknowledgments

Thank you to the contributing authors who shared their resilience stories: Dr. Yvonne Kaye, Dr. Anna Margolina, Dr. Larissa Chuprina, Ron Harrell, Gary B. Larson, Marcelle Allen, Edie Weinstein, Rocky Kandola, Dara Lee, and Frank King.

Thank you to Douglas Schmidt for giving permission to share his beautiful wife Maria Salomoa Schmidt's story.

Thank you to Mary Bain for allowing me to tell her story and to Lauren Nelson, for graciously giving permission to tell her story before her passing.

Thank you to the wonderful authors and colleagues who gave advance reviews and cover quotes for this book: Alex Montoya, Dr. Lise Deguire, Dr. Katherine T. Kelly, Dr. Yvonne Kaye, and Debbie Hampton, Anne Hunter Logue, Kathleen Ritter, Dr. Larissa Chuprina, Thomas E. Ziemann, and Rev. Edie Weinstein.

Thank you to the practitioners who shared their generous healing gifts: Dr. Anna Margolina, Dr. Katherine T. Kelly, Bill Protzmann and Dr. Yvonne Kaye.

A big thank you to Victor Perton for writing the Foreword and his kind, wise and optimistic words.

Thank you to Lisa Robinson, Moon Cat Studio, for cover design.

Thank you finally to Pierucci Publishing and the team who helped to bring this book to life.

Kate Olson, November 2021

Contents

A Note to the Readers..11

Foreword... 13

Introduction... 17

PART 1 - The "Why?" 23

Chapter One: How Are Resilience & Joyful Resilience Different?.......24

Chapter Two: Can You Be Joyful in the Midst of Adversity?..............36

Chapter Three: Can Resilience Be Learned,
Replicated & Expanded? 44

Chapter Four: What Are the Traits of Resilience?.............................55

Chapter Five: The History Behind Resilience....................................63

Chapter Six: Clearing Limiting Beliefs & Energy Blocks.....................70

PART 2 – Stories of Resilience -The Inspiration.........81

Chapter Seven: My Stories Learning Resilience...................82

Chapter Eight: Resilience Learned from Friends 99

Chapter Nine: The Resilience of Immigrants 112

Chapter Ten: The Resilience of Men...............................126

Chapter Eleven: The Resilience of Women........................143

PART 3 – The "How?" 157

Chapter Twelve: Creating Mindset...................................158

Chapter Thirteen: Resilience Practices, Routines & Activities..........169

Chapter Fourteen: Resilience Exercises & Tools 184

Chapter Fifteen: Final Thoughts & Gifts...........................205

About the Author..219

A Note to the Readers

Living in Joyful Resilience: A Roadmap for Navigating Life's Ups & Downs is meant to bring about awareness as to what joyful resilience is and how it is different from simply being resilient. I will demonstrate to you through my stories, the stories of the contributors and the information I provide on how our mind, emotions and the brain work to become both more joyful and more resilient. The practices, exercises and tools are to guide you on your continuing journey building and constantly strengthening your own joyful resilience. This is not something you will do once and then you're done and forever joyfully resilient. It is a continuing journey of strengthening and honing your skills, traits, and mindset. It is a process of making yourself into your own champion and resilient   superhero. The journey is never truly over, but if you work on it, there will come a time when you know whatever adversity life brings, you are ready and will rise above it, to bounce back joyfully.

When you understand how the mind, body and emotions work together, you can better do what is needed to get the results you want. The accompanying journal, *Simple Soul Thoughts: Collecting Moments of Joy*, will help you in building your mindset, getting to know yourself better, and becoming more aware of your thoughts and feelings. More awareness will help you in building many of the other traits that make you stronger, more adaptable, and happier. The opportunity to reflect on your thoughts and feelings is valuable insight for making changes when needed and recognizing patterns that are not serving you. The gifts in the final chapter of the book are an awesome bonus that will help you in many ways!

Be sure to download them! I was so honored to have these amazing healers share their beautiful gifts with you. You don't just have me in your corner cheering you on - there are a whole team of people wishing you joyful resilience and offering you needed resources to enhance your life and help you get there! Now, let's hit the road and start navigating past those obstacles and bumps in life's highway to joyfulness!

Foreword

Today, I walked into the State Rose Garden not far from my home In Melbourne, Australia. As I walked through the gate, the breeze brought me the intoxicating perfume of a thousand roses of many hues. It was a joyful way to start my day.

So too, this evening, it is a joy to share my insights on Kate Olson's book, *Living in Joyful Resilience: A Roadmap for Navigating Life's Ups & Downs*.

Kate has shared her passion for what she has learned about living in joyful resilience. She offers practical habits that we can all adopt.

Kate writes, "Building resilience and joyful resilience is a matter of habit and practice."

My experience of living in leadership and serving leaders led me to establish the Centre for Optimism. My belief is that everyone is a leader at some time, and I urge my audiences to graffiti their mirror at home and work with my affirmation, "The leader looks like the person in my mirror."

My motivation was that much of the good in the world is obscured by a fog of pessimism and negativity. The 2020s and pandemic led people to a yearning for stories of hope. The leaders they want to follow are realistic and infectiously optimistic.

As Kate says, we must each follow our own path. The only person we can change is ourselves. I ask, "What makes YOU optimistic?" of people of all walks of life globally.

Hence the admiration I feel for Kate's mission in joyful resilience.

Like Kate, the first two habits I commend to people are to make sure they smile and laugh more. Smile at everyone and share your joy. Laugh more, whether jokes, watching comedy, engaging in laughter yoga, or just laughing because it feels good.

Kate suggests we forest bathe and coincidentally, last weekend I joined friends for a Utopia Retreat in the Australian bush and went forest bathing by the Little Yarra River. The sound of the babbling brook accompanied by the laughter of the kookaburras still resonates and makes me smile, filling me with joy.

Meditation is a crucial recommendation of Kate's and I agree. During presentations for large audiences, I share a Loving-Kindness Meditation. This morning as I woke, I did a simple meditation focusing on the breath passing through my nostrils and I remained energized hours later.

Joyful Resilience

In her book, Kate lists optimism as one of the seven "super power" traits of joyful resilience. Optimism certainly is an underpinning trait of resilience. How can you persist if you don't think persistence will yield a better future?

One of the ancients who influenced me was Mother Julian of Norwich. In her book, *The Revelations of Divine Love*, Julian says, "All shall be well, all shall be well, all manner of thing shall be well."

That message resonates hundreds of years later in the contemporary definition of optimism. At its simplest, optimism is an expectation that good things will happen and that things will work out in the end. And if they have not worked, it's not the end.

Forming new habits isn't easy, so I encourage doing It joyfully as Kate says, with actions that bring you enjoyment. I have Pharrell's "Happy" on my optimism playlist and I often dance with the video version of the song. "Dancing in the Street" is a favorite song and a favorite thing to do!

One of my favorite habits is the Gratitude Habit. At the end of the day, set aside time to journal the three best things in the day and send thank you messages to people who made you smile. A key to the success of this habit is reading, the next morning, what you wrote the night before. *The Simple Soul Thoughts: Collecting Moments of Joy* journal that accompanies Kate's book, is perfect for this.

I love Kate's mission of sharing the habits and wisdom of joyful resilience.

Joyful resilience and optimism are mindset choices you make every day. I align with Kate in asking you to join us in encouraging joyful resilience and spreading optimism daily.

Victor Perton, November 22, 2021

Victor is the founder & CEO of the Centre for Optimism, barrister, former ambassador to the USA, leadership advocate, speaker, and author of The Case for Optimism: The Optimist's Voices and Optimism: The How and Why.

Links for *Soul Fire Wisdom* Interviews with Victor:

"A Case for Optimism," December, 2019,
https://www.youtube.com/watch?v=R8V8X5Hd2fc

"Is Optimism on the Rise?" December, 2020,
https://www.youtube.com/watch?v=QS7H77tu62I

Introduction

It is profoundly relevant that I moved from Washington State to Arizona as I embarked on writing this book. There is no greater example of strength and resilience in nature than the desert, and there is no better teacher about life and living than nature. In its brilliance, nature demonstrates how bending saves us from breaking and finding a new path allows us to move forward. Nature shows us that it is possible to break through and grow in situations that might look impossible. Going through the experience of big changes during the chaos and uncertainty of the COVID-19 pandemic was also highly enlightening. From the beginning, I viewed the move as an adventure, although it offered me a good share of obstacles, adversity, and some degree of pain and discomfort, I still see it as an adventure and lesson-filled gift.

Living in Joyful Resilience: A Roadmap to Navigating Life's Ups & Downs explains the difference between resilience and joyful resilience, outlines the traits and skill sets of resilience, gives you helpful steps for changing your mindset to become both more resilient and more joyful, shares insightful stories of resilience that will motivate and inspire you, gives practices, exercises and tools to strengthen and expand your joy and resilience, and provides resources for further development on your joyful resilience journey. You will have the tools you need for a happier, healthier life and the ability to meet life's challenges and demands head-on with the confidence that you will not only bounce back but bounce forward and achieve your greatest aspirations.

It is well-known that resilience is a needed quality to successfully navigate times of great change and enlightenment, and we are certainly experiencing those times now in so many ways. Lastly, the optional accompanying journal will help you to build your reservoir of joyfulness, make you aware of the many blessings already in your life and help to attract more joy and blessings to you. The bonus gifts at the end of the book are helpful additional tools and resources that will enrich your experience.

Living in Joyful Resilience: A Roadmap for Navigating Life's Ups & Downs is a book that was on my agenda for quite some time. I thought it was important to share the experience I had in discovering that suffering and sadness need not be a constant state of being while we encounter obstacles, adversity, and very difficult times. I did not think it would be my first book, as I had some other projects on my agenda ahead of it. However, 2020 and the COVID-19 pandemic changed that, I could see no greater need in these times than for resilience, and specifically, *joyful resilience.*

In the course of talking with a friend and colleague, we agreed that the quality of *joyful resilience* was both highly relevant and much needed by everyone in our current times. My colleague Dr. Chuprina, an immigrant herself, has helped immigrants on their journey of adapting successfully into a new culture. She brought up that there is a lot of resilience both needed and demonstrated in the process that immigrants experience.

I told Dr. Chuprina that I had witnessed the quality of resilience strongly present in immigrants that I met as well. We decided to do a "Soul Talk" on this topic. *Soul Talks* is a video blog I do and have available for viewing on my websites, with conversations on pre-selected topics. This talk, and responses to it, further inspired my desire to write the book at this time, to provide a resource with the hope that it will be a helpful tool for facing adversity and developing that reserve that helps us become joyfully resilient. Listen to our Soul Talk on YouTube.com: https://youtu.be/vpq5RMtUYXk

Scan or take a photo of this QR Code to enjoy our Soul Talk on YouTube.

I have always been resilient. It was modeled for me in my childhood and required of me in my family. My childhood showed me obstacles and adversities, and I was taught to cope with difficulties and rise above them. It was a part of every aspect of my upbringing, from Catholic school and Church to the way my parents dealt with life, as well as the norms and mores of my social environment and the times I grew up in. The resilience I knew, though, was born of suffering and sadness. It wasn't only hard to develop this resilience, as anyone would expect, but it was veritably spirit-crushing. I did not know there was any other way for a long time.

My mother was sick throughout my entire childhood, and that required me to bear more responsibility than children usually do. My father was an alcoholic, which had its own set of difficulties. I did, however, discover that resilience does not have to be governed by suffering and sadness, but that it can be rooted in *joyfulness*.

This is where my motivation for writing this book originated. I came to know that we can be joyful, even in the face of those adversities that inalterably changed my own life and outlook, even from a young age. I hope to convey what I have learned about living in joyful resilience to you so that you will be stronger and happier too. The accompanying journal, which you can purchase with, *Living in Joyful Resilience*, is designed to help you create that core of joyfulness that builds stronger resilience and gives us a happier, healthier life in the process.

Did you hear about the rose that grew
from a crack in the concrete?
Proving nature's law is wrong it
Learned to walk without having feet.
Funny it seems, but by keeping its dreams,
It learned to breathe fresh air.
Long live the rose that grew from concrete
When no one else ever cared.
– Tupac Shakur

Part One

The "Why?"

In Chapters One through Six, I set the framework for this book and answer the questions:

*What is the difference between resilience and **joyful resilience?***

*Why is **joyful resilience** important?*

*How does **joyful resilience** affect our lives and the way we navigate obstacles and adversity?*

Chapter One

"The human capacity for burden is like bamboo – far more flexible than you'd ever believe at first glance."

– Jodi Picoult

How is Joyful Resilience Different from Resilience?

What is Resilience?

Resilience, simply defined, is that driving force that leads us to persevere and rise above or bounce back from adversity. It is the quality that leads us to heal wounds and overcome the obstacles we encounter. It is the force that makes us keep going and not quit.

According to Wikipedia, psychological resilience is:

Psychological resilience is the ability to mentally or emotionally cope with a crisis or to return to pre-crisis status quickly. Resilience exists when the person uses mental processes and behaviors in promoting personal assets and protecting self from the potential negative effects of stressors.

Some people see resilience as mental toughness and the ability to stay the course, no matter what obstacles are encountered, and then to overcome and achieve your goals. Resilience can, however, be physical, mental, emotional, and psychological in nature, as well. Resilience is not a single trait, but a set of traits or skill sets that one draws upon to deal with stressors brought on by adversities.

What is Joyful Resilience?

Joyful resilience is all of the above traits but includes a mindset or attitude component that not only strengthens its effects and consequent outcomes but has an enduring effect on our brains; resilience makes us stronger, more resourceful, and more able to rise above future adversities. This component is the ability to return to and maintain a core state of joy or joyfulness.

Resilience literally rewires our brains in a positive way that leads to better emotional stability and well-being. It changes the way we respond to adversity and the outcomes that we get from the actions we take. It also simply feels better and allows us to be better versions of ourselves. These might seem like big claims, but I will break down how joyful resilience or joy itself, as a component of resilience, works.

Joy is a powerful mindset and emotional state. It can make a huge difference to our outlook and perceptions. Joyful resilience has both physiological and neurological effects that make all the other traits and components of resilience more powerful. I will talk more about the components of joyful resilience and the neuroscience explanation of how things work in later chapters.

Brené Brown has described joy and its relationship to resilience this way:

> *"Joy, collected over time, fuels resilience – ensuring we'll have reservoirs of emotional strength when hard things do happen."*

I am quoting her for the second time here because I want those words to sink in and really make an impact. They are powerful and say more than you might first think. Realizing that our emotions, thoughts, and perceptions act as fuel or food for how our body and mind function and respond to everything is both logical and so unexpectedly empowering.

There are many components that make up resilience with joy being the primary differentiating component between mere resilience and *joyful resilience*. We will discuss the traits that make up resilience, as well as how to cultivate and strengthen those characteristics within yourself. Building resilience and *joyful resilience* is a matter of habit and practice. Like most other skills in life, we constantly become better at *joyful resilience* with focus and intention, as well as the experience offered by overcoming adversities, which equates to practice.

What Are The Characteristics Of Resilience?

Not everyone agrees on the specific characteristics that a person needs to be resilient, and some people break it down into different categories of resilience as well, such as emotional, spiritual, strategic, and so on. I am presenting resilience in a broader sense and I'm listing here the qualities that generally will help a person to be more resilient in all potential circumstances. I am taking a broader look than most academic studies do and feel that, in practice, they are all integrated in a practical sense.

- Awareness / insight
- Resourcefulness
- Problem-solving
- Perseverance
- Confidence or self-esteem
- Adaptability
- Hope
- Optimism
- Creativity
- Self-control
- Calmness
- Determination
- Empathy
- Sense of humor
- Forgiveness
- Compassion
- Gratitude
- Faith or belief

- Support / community
- Self-love

If you add joy or joyfulness to these traits and skills, you have *joyful resilience.* Joy or joyfulness can be defined as a state of being or mindset where great happiness, delight, pleasure, and bliss are experienced on a frequent and consistent basis. As Brené Brown said above, when we store away the collection of small joys in our daily lives, we build a reservoir of joyfulness, which buoys us up through times of adversity.

Not all of the traits above are required for a person to be resilient, however, the more of these you have and draw upon, the more resilient you become.

This is why resilience is something you can build and strengthen on a continuing basis as you develop more of the traits and characteristics that support this mindset. I will talk more about the individual traits and why they contribute to resilience, as well as how to cultivate them.

There is a story from my childhood I sometimes tell. It was both an important lesson on resilience and made me very aware of the overwhelming power of joy. My memory is of first grade at Catholic school and reading aloud from our readers. Learning to read did not come easily to me at first, though I quickly came to love it. Reading was a challenge, as I was slightly dyslexic and very shy, so reading aloud was especially difficult. My teacher, Sister Mary of the Divine Heart, was pretty strict, and she demanded perfection. We were expected to volunteer to read or she would call on us. We were awarded gold stars for our performance. They were put in neat rows in the front of our readers. The best reader for the day was selected to put the stars in the books, and it was an honor to be chosen. It was a big deal and I wanted more than anything to have those gold stars and to be the person to put them in the books, but I was too afraid to volunteer. One day I was chosen to read and was finally picked to put the stars in the books. I was so excited! Perhaps I was overexcited because things got out of hand; I got a little carried away with the stars. I not only put a star in my book and everyone else's book, as I was supposed to do, but I put lots of stars in my book and everyone else's. Everyone seemed very happy with the extra stars and so was I. I still remember the proud, beaming little faces, and I remember looking at those neat little rows of stars feeling proud, confident, and, well, a kind of satisfaction that was simply empowering!

It was pure joy!

When I went home that night, my mom noticed all the extra stars and, after some coaxing, I was forced to tell her about getting carried away and putting more stars than I was supposed to in my book and everyone else's. She seemed to understand but insisted that I tell Sister Mary first thing the next morning. My mom told me that the gold stars were nice, but that I should know that I was reading my very best, whether I got a gold star or not, and that I should read well enough every day to deserve all those gold stars. I promised her and myself that I would. When I told Sister Mary what I had done, she was not happy and told me that I would never again get to give out the stars. I had to stay after school for several days and write my name on the board, which was a punishment, kind of a "shame" listing.

Strangely, this did not deter my determination to prove that I deserved all those gold stars; from then on, I volunteered to read every day and knew that I read very well. I also noticed the smiles from everyone when I read and that they too seemed to read with more confidence. I always wondered if they were earning their stars too and if Sister Mary noticed the special "magic" that those gold stars seemed to have? Yes, I knew that I had been wrong in not following directions and getting carried away with the stars. I blamed it on the "magic" of those shiny gold stars. Going forward, gold stars have always had the effect of making me feel joyful and I think a little more confident, courageous, and resilient.

This event was brought to mind when I was presenting a speech for the Symposium for Personal Development, held at the Harvard Faculty Club in Cambridge, MA, in 2016. It was an honor I almost passed on due to my great fear of public speaking. I decided to do it, but as I listened to the polished and eloquently delivered talks of my colleagues, I was getting more anxious and fearful. Then an amazing lady stepped onto the stage with more enthusiasm and exuberance than I had ever seen. Her name was Shiny Burcu Unsal, and she is often referred to as "The Shiny One." She is an amazing, speaker, author, coach, and NLP trainer. Her talk was entertaining and informative, but what made the biggest impact on me was that she was decorated in colorful stars, and she graciously distributed more to all the audience members.

Shiny's stars brought back for me that decades-old memory of joyfulness and mastery over my fears, so as I stepped on the stage, with the gold and silver stars on my hand, the courage to push past my fears came to me. I gave my presentation on "The Simple Grace of Embracing Change." This is how powerful those pieces of joy we hold in our memory can be!

There are many guides or examples of resilience in our leaders and the famous people we revere. Most of them have many of the traits I mentioned, and the ones that really stand out also have that quality or characteristic of joyfulness as part of their resilience story. Some that come to mind for me are Nelson Mandela, Mahala Yousafzai, Mother Teresa, Mahatma Gandhi, Oprah, Rosa Parks, John McCain, John F. Kennedy, J.K. Rowling, and Michael Jordan. They were all resilient in different ways, at different times, and joyfulness was an important part of their resilience and success in overcoming adversity in each case. They were all people who persevered and maintained a positive and optimistic outlook. They held on to joys and grew stronger through experiencing adversities, each in their individual way.

There are so many other examples to be held up; if they can persevere so can we all. The beauty of *joyful resilience* is that as hard as things may get at times, and as difficult as it might seem, anything done in joy feels so much better than anything done through struggle and suffering.

Imagine a bitter and vengeful Nelson Mandela. How would that have worked? I don't think he would have achieved nearly as much or impacted so many people in South Africa and around the world, so profoundly, if he had done so with a negative mindset. It might have destroyed him rather than making him such a resilient and respected leader.

Resilience without joy may get you through obstacles, adversities, and difficult times, however, it has a different effect on you both mentally and emotionally. It affects your brain differently and, therefore, your future reactions and ability to be resilient in new situations. Think of it this way: when you go through a situation where all you have known is suffering and sadness, even if you get through it and survive, your primary reaction, when confronted with a similar situation, is dread and foreboding. You really don't want to do it again; you see it only as hard and filled with pain and suffering. You are naturally focused on that pain and suffering, rather than any potential upside, lesson, or gift that might be received.

However, if you go through that situation and there is an element of joyfulness in it, or perhaps you experience learning in this adversity; the adversity is still difficult, you may hope you will not encounter it again, however, there is a greater chance that you will be able to handle the situation and move into it more confidently.

If there were moments of joy, pleasure, or happiness that you experienced along the way, your brain is more willing to jump in and tackle things again. That small difference in mental outlook or mindset is crucial, and your brain is in a different state of being when you maintain those moments of joy.

Joy or happiness has a different effect than does devastation, suffering, and sadness. The chemicals emitted are different and the way your brain connects and rewires itself is different. Suffering and sadness form different patterns in your brain than happiness and joy and they give you different resources to draw on the next time around. The brain constantly replicates established patterns resulting in repeating responses. That is just how it works. Fortunately, you do have control over this. It is solely a matter of choosing your thoughts and emotions to change the patterns and thus, changing the way you are going to respond to obstacles and adversity in the future.

This is why it is better to be joyfully resilient than to be simply resilient.

How possible and realistic is it though? You are instinctively called on to be resilient when things are difficult or challenging. Is it really possible to experience joy through those hard times? I think it is and Ernest Hemingway thought so too:

"The world breaks everyone, and afterward, some are strong at the broken places."

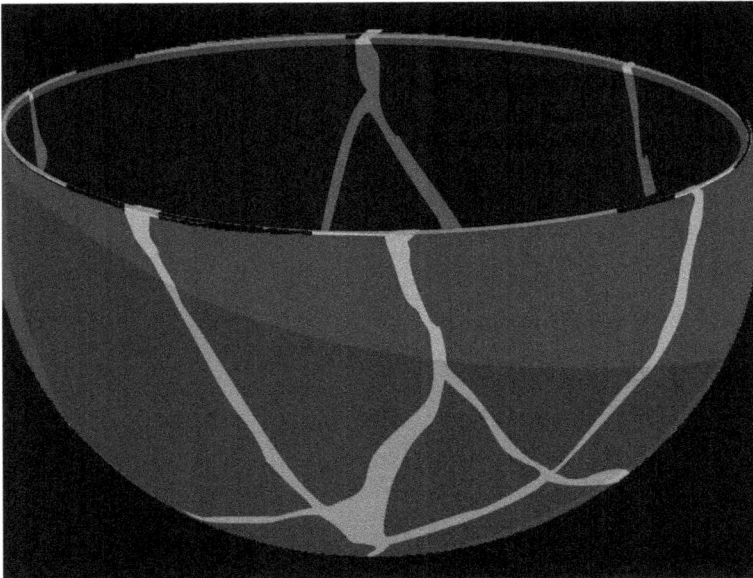

In Japan, they have an art form where broken pottery is glued together and painted with glorious and luxurious gold. It is called *Kintsugi*. It is creating beauty from broken pieces and evokes the connection between joy and resilience. You do have that ability to experience joy through the worst of times, even the ones that break you emotionally into pieces. You have the ability to heal, to learn, to pull yourself together, and to be beautifully whole and functional again.

Your resilience is a magnificent force and gift to your human functioning and existence.

When you add joyfulness to resilience it becomes an even stronger, more empowering force. Joy is more than just momentary happiness. It is a state of being and mindset that is created by your focus on awareness and appreciation in the present moment, acknowledgment of the blessings and comforts, and delight and pleasure in the small things that are part of our daily lives. It is seeing with a deep and constant sense of gratitude. As you cultivate these small joyful moments, they become a habit, an outlook, a state of being, to which you constantly return through the myriad of emotions that you experience in response to the circumstances of life, positive or negative. This core of joyfulness becomes the comfort zone you seek to return to and focus your energy toward. You look for the joy in every circumstance and are more likely to find some joy in everything you encounter, no matter how small.

In the most severe circumstances, it is the small joys that have gotten people through. This ability to seek, find or recognize these small joys and focus on them is a primary quality in being highly resilient. If you talk with survivors of abuse, war, captivity, great loss, catastrophic illness, injury, and other extreme adversities, most will tell you about the small joys that got them through those experiences and buoyed up their spirits, motivating them to keep going. They remember those small joys more readily than the details of the adversity they faced.

Neuroscience explains it this way: happiness or joy is a survival mechanism. This is because, in the presence of something positive, something we like, or something that feels good, our brain releases four main "feel-good" chemicals. These chemicals are endorphin, oxytocin, serotonin, and dopamine. The chemicals have significant effects on your body, your brain, your mood, and your emotions. They quite literally affect every cell in your body. Physically, they make you stronger, keep you healthier, and even make you look better. Mentally, they help the circuits in your brain connect, making you quicker and better able to think and reason. Emotionally, they make you feel calmer, more in control, and give you a sense of tranquility and balance. All of these chemical responses make you more resilient to any obstacles or adversities that you might encounter. Joy and happiness don't just feel good, they make your body and mind function better and that makes you more resourceful in finding ways to deal with adversities.

"We cannot cure the world of sorrows, but we can choose to live in joy."

– Joseph Campbell

Chapter Two

"The knowledge that you have emerged wiser and stronger from setbacks means that you are ever after, secure in your ability to survive."

— J. K Rowling

Can You Be Joyful in the Amidst of Adversity?

Through difficult times we must be resilient. Twenty-twenty and the persistent pandemic have certainly given us a lesson in the need for resilience. The question is—must our resilience be full of pain, sadness, and suffering? There was much in that year-plus, of course, about which we feel great sadness, even defeat, and grief. There was great pain and, yes, many suffered great loss. This has included a previously unimaginable loss of lives, loss of jobs, loss of businesses, loss of income, loss of aspirations, dreams, and everyday life experiences. Additionally, people have been disconnected, isolated, lonely, and uncertain, which caused extreme levels of stress and anxiety.

Despite all of this, there were good moments, benefits, and silver linings. There was and is so much that we can still appreciate and be thankful for. There was and is still hope for better days to come, belief that we will overcome our obstacles and adversities, present and future, and again enjoy experiencing some of what has been lost during these times.

Is it possible to remain joyful and experience happiness, even in the worst of times? When things are really bad, when you are in the throes of true disaster and adversity, experiencing illness, loss, grief, and/or you are seriously concerned about very real survival needs? Is it still possible to be joyful and feel generally happy most of the time?

If it is possible, is this a desirable state? Or are we just ignoring the stark reality confronting us?

It is not only possible, but it is how you get through bad times in the most resilient and healthy way to avoid many damaging side effects to your physical and emotional long-term health. It is how you stay sane, maintain the best mindset, and how you become most resourceful in resolving issues or finding solutions to problems that may arise.

This has been demonstrated to us by many who have experienced extreme adversity and yet maintained a joyful attitude through their circumstances. They would have described themselves as generally happy, even when also experiencing and feeling great suffering. The examples are many including Holocaust survivors and veterans of war; survivors of abuse, violence, devastating accidents, and illness; as well as people like Nelson Mandela, Malala Yousafzai, Mother Theresa, Mahatma

Gandhi, and others mentioned in the previous chapter; and many, many more. These are people who have gone through things most of us cannot imagine surviving and have done so maintaining their joyful resilience. There are also many everyday heroes among us, who have quietly endured and survived the worst and gone on to live happy, joyful lives.

We are told it is not good to avoid our feelings and that we must experience them. When something really devastating is happening or has happened, how can we be anything but sad, unhappy, and dwell in those feelings? We must experience our feelings, however, we need not dwell in them. That is really it. We can experience more than just one feeling.

In each moment we experience a particular feeling and acknowledge it, we need to do that, but from moment to moment our feelings and what we allow ourselves to experience can change. It is okay to experience the full and changing range of our emotions and that is the healthiest way to deal with them. You can be very sad and truly feel a loss and still a short time later experience a moment of joy when your pet or your partner snuggles up to you. You can be feeling very lonely in one moment and then feel joy when a funny movie or something in real life makes you laugh. It is when you try to dwell in a single emotion and not experience the full range of your emotions that you become stuck in unhappiness, grief, depression, or sadness, and rob yourself of the joy that is still there for you in living life moment to moment.

The times we are living in now are truly devastating in so many ways. They are quite uncertain, with the only certainty being that COVID-19 is impacting us in ways that will forever change us. Death is imminent, but we seem closer to it; the threat feels more real. There is a real danger to our health and there are challenges that affect our emotional and financial well-being. There are concerns bombarding us from every direction. Many people have been and continue to be seriously worried about our political division and the circumstances our country has recently gone through. At the same time, there are the usual adversities of life happening in our individual lives.

A friend of mine died of brain cancer this summer, and I couldn't even go see him because of the virus and hospital regulations. There are people who are homeless and hungry in epidemic proportions. In fact, I saw a terrible accident yesterday and could only wonder what dealing with that would be like for those involved. Still, I am enjoying the beautiful weather we are having here today in Southern Arizona.

And I am allowed, even in these times, to appreciate and feel joy. I felt a sense of peace and joy, as I always do, being outdoors and watching a beautiful sunset over the lake. I try to do a couple of small things daily that bring me joy. I start the day listening to music and that always brightens my spirits. I rewarded myself with a very decadent chocolate dessert and a glass of wine yesterday while watching a romantic comedy. It was totally silly! I laughed and loved it.

I savored those feelings and that is okay, even though it still breaks my heart that a good friend I care about passed away too young and I couldn't say goodbye in person or give him one last hug and tell him how much he meant to me. Yes, I feel that sadness deeply, but I can also feel gratitude, appreciation, and happiness. I can feel the honor that it was to know him, the light he brought to my life, and gratitude for our friendship. I catch myself worrying about something from time to time and I try to switch it up quickly after asking myself if there is anything that I can do about it right now. I try to stay in the moment and take care of myself, as I would anyone else that I love. I try to be intentional in what I do, stay connected to my family, my friends, and those who add positivity and light to my life.

You know, even in these difficult times, I smile often, I see a lot of good in the world and much to be grateful for. I feel joyful and happy most of the time despite all the chaos of this very long year-plus of adversity and loss with the COVID-19 pandemic and, for that, I am truly and abundantly grateful! Life is good and the best is still yet to come! We can absolutely be joyful in the midst of adversity!

This is important to realize and a crucial part of the mindset of joyful resilience. We sometimes think that we must dwell in a single emotion to feel it sufficiently and are reluctant to move on or forward not realizing that it is entirely possible to experience more than one emotion and that you do not have to entirely give one emotion up to feel another. You can put it on the back burner, so to speak, while you take a moment to feel and appreciate something else, another important feeling that should not be ignored.

Some people feel guilty about letting go of an emotion, even temporarily, when it involves a loved one, but we don't need to.

Our emotions are moment to moment. Some things may take time to work through, such as grief, but we do not have to dwell in them every moment of our being. This is one of the lessons in mindfulness: being present in the moment, feeling it fully, then moving on to the next. To have joy or happiness as your core state of being, you do not have to be happy or joyful every moment. That would actually be impossible. You just have to be fully present in those moments of joy you do experience and return to that state on a regular and continuing basis.

When I started my first radio show, *Embrace Change with Kate*, one of my first guests was Debbie Hampton. I had connected with her on LinkedIn, where I saw articles she had posted, then on Facebook, and eventually I read her book, *Beat Depression and Anxiety by Changing Your Brain: With Simple Practices that Will Improve Your Life*. I was so inspired by her story and her resilience that I had to interview her. I can't tell her whole story here, but Debbie went through a battle with anxiety and depression over unresolved traumas and losses that led her to a suicide attempt, leaving her with a traumatic brain injury. She is not a therapist or a coach, but a writer, and in her very inspiring struggle and journey back to reclaiming her brain function, mental and physical health, and her life, she learned much about mental health and studied neuroscience very extensively. Her story, what she learned and now shares through her book and articles, is relevant because she confirms much of what is just observed or studied by others, through her own experience. Moreover, she very beautifully and clearly describes things with her uncomplicated writing style. In her book, Debbie says this:

41

"Being brain injured showed the pain which had piled up over the years before the suicide attempt, finally causing me to crumble under its weight, was totally in my thoughts. -- What it really boiled down to was making the decision not to do that to myself anymore. -- These days, I remind myself to think of and put my energy into possibilities, not problems: past, present, or future. This doesn't mean that I ignore reality and live in an illusory world filled with sunshine all the time. It means that I acknowledge and accept what is: good and bad, consider my possible options, consequences, and outcomes, and choose to focus my energy on creating positive while being prepared to respond (not react) to whatever arises and work with it for my good. I'd rather take a risk than have regrets. In instead of asking "Why?" I ask "Why not?"

Debbie's story is an important example; she is one of those everyday heroes and her study into neuroscience and recovery story is an education in resilience in itself.

J.K. Rowling is another great example of someone who learned to live with *joyful resilience* and, I would guess, she still does.

"Rock bottom became a solid foundation on which I rebuilt my life."

- J.K. Rowling

"Happiness can be found in the darkest of times, if one only remembers to turn on the light."

- J.K. Rowling

It is not necessary to experience the depression, suicide attempt, and brain injury that Debbie Hampton valiantly struggled back from, the destitution that J. K. Rowling experienced, or to rise to the fame and fortune that she has been blessed with, for all the above statements to be true for you. Rowling expresses, in her wise and eloquent words, some universal truths about joy and resilience. Read her words again and take them to heart, they will provide a good foundation for building your own joyful resilience.

Chapter Three

"It's your reaction to adversity, not adversity itself that determines how life's story will develop."

— Dieter F. Uchtdorf

Can Resilience Be Learned, Replicated & Expanded?

To be sustainable, something must be able to be maintained and continued. In terms of this characteristic of *joyful resilience*, it would mean that we can be joyfully resilient today and it can be replicated in the future.

It is common knowledge that life-changing experiences in our human development require resilience or the ability to restore yourself after a crisis or even to become stronger and better. Resilience building seems to come from either a catastrophic event or a chain of dramatic life events that require us to respond and, in the process, build skills and attitudes that can be described as resilience. These are skills that have durability and give us the ability to last and to bounce back after overcoming difficulty. Sometimes, we might leap forward and achieve a higher level of resilience than where we were previously. Many times, this involves releasing ourselves from fear of failure and having the courage to take a risk.

I believe that resilience has several components: knowledge, skills, traits, and attitude or mindset, that are built and strengthened over time. While knowledge and skills are teachable, mindset can be created, changed, or shifted by experience or coaching when someone does the inner work.

Mindset is the most needed change, yet the most challenging. While resilience or *joyful resilience* mindset can be created and grown, conversely, it has also been found in research studies that there is a breaking point for almost everyone and that resilience can break down and diminish as well. Below are some recommendations for preventing the breakdown of resilience and creating a joyful and positive mindset that helps to sustain the ability to bounce back from adversity:

- Empathizing with others experiencing hardships
- Showing kindness to others
- Looking inward rather than outward for happiness
- Realizing that all things are temporary including suffering and adversity
- Having human connections including relationships and community (even pets can be
- helpful)

- Practices like meditation and yoga that use focus and breathing
- Exercise and physical activities that keep our body moving
- Being outdoors and experiencing nature
- Gratitude and appreciation for the experience of life
- Avoiding a state of upset, anger, worry, or excessive complaining
- A sense of purpose
- An optimistic outlook
- Creative activities of all types
- Working with coaches, teachers, or practitioners for help figuring things out
- Setting and achieving new goals

Learning to Be More Resilient

Resilience as a concept was first introduced into the vocabulary in the 17th century and has been defined in different ways over time since then. It has only been during the 20th century going forward, however, that resilience and learning resilience or what is called "resilience theory" have been significantly studied.

In the past forty to fifty years there have been significant strides in resilience study and research, tying together multiple disciplines, coming up with findings that are changing the way we look at resilience. It has been determined that resilience can be learned in multiple ways and that resilience can be taught. Several studies over the past seventy years have followed participants over spans of thirty to forty years noting traits, experiences, and outcomes of internal, external, and environmental stressors and their effects and outcomes regarding the learning and teaching of resilience.

In an article in the *New Yorker*, "How People Learn To Be Resilient" (February 11, 2016) Maria Konnikova outlines some of the foremost research and studies over the past decades, and some of the conclusions that have evolved from those studies.

- One key study she cites and draws reference from in her article is Emmy Werner (1989) a developmental psychologist who followed a group of 698 children for their response to stressors before birth for thirty-two years.
- Norman Garmezy (1999) a developmental psychologist and clinician at the University of Minnesota studied thousands of children over four decades trying to determine the factors that made some children more resilient than others found that this resilience factor was learned.
- George Bonanno, a clinical psychologist at Columbia University's teacher's college and head of the Loss, Trauma and Emotion Lab, has been studying resilience for the past twenty-five years.
- And finally, Konnikova cites Martin Seligman, a psychologist at the University of Pennsylvania and pioneer in the field of positive psychology.

Let's dive into these studies and their most important takeaways.

Konnikova draws out some turning point conclusions from these researchers and their studies that point to resilience being both learnable and teachable. In addition, Konnikova's analysis supports my theory that joyfulness as an underpinning attitude or mindset is an important factor in building resilience.

In their extensive studies, both Werner and Garmezy discovered that not all at-risk children reacted to stressors in the same way. While both discovered that there were several factors that determined which children were more resilient, there were a couple of things that stood out in those that were the most resilient.

One was how the children saw themselves with regard to having control over their own lives or what is sometimes referred to as "locus of control." The term "locus of control" is commonly used in research studies and refers to an individual's perception of the causes of events that affect them. Do they see themselves as having some effect or control over events, or do they see it as out of their hands and up to some external force, such as fate, God, or other powers? Another strong indicator discovered was a support system of someone: a parent, teacher, community, or other support system offering resources and guidance.

Garmezy is largely credited with further defining and changing the focus of the study to the quality that has come to be known as resilience. He saw resilience as the adaption to succeed despite adversity and life stressors. He looked for the positive qualities and strengths that allowed some to rise above adversities and succeed. Prior studies had focused more on the vulnerabilities and weaknesses that made people unable to succeed or be resilient. Garmezy studied thousands of children and saw many cases wherein, despite circumstances, children rose above their adversities to succeed and thrive. One case that made a big impact on him, which he subsequently talked about in interviews, was about a boy who came from a family with an alcoholic mother and an absent father. The mother could barely support the boy still, it was important to the boy that, "no one would pity him and no one would know the ineptitude of his mother." He felt it was up to him to control this, so every day he arrived at school with a big smile on his face and a bread sandwich tucked in his lunch bag. He excelled academically and went on to become a successful, stable adult, despite his unfortunate circumstances. This, Garmezy concluded, is resilience.

The research of Bonanno and Seligman further identified what makes some people more resilient than others when we are all operating with the same set of functional systems to respond to life stressors. Bonanno concluded that perceptions, not the actual circumstances, are largely determinate of who is resilient and to what degree. Bonanno said, "Events are not traumatic until we experience them as traumatic." Therefore, two people may experience the same circumstance and one may be traumatized by it and the other may not. This is largely a result of how each of them perceived what they experienced and not the circumstances themselves. This puts resilience in a whole new light and opens the door to validating my observations of the power of *joyful resilience* and the impact of mindset in general. This has been further studied and validated in the fields of positive psychology and neuroscience.

Joyful Resilience & Neuroscience

Neuroscience is one of the newer fields of study that is explaining a lot about how our brains work and how resilience and *joyful resilience* can be learned and taught. According to Wikipedia, neuroscience is:

> the scientific study of the nervous system. It is a multidisciplinary science that combines physiology, anatomy, molecular biology, developmental biology, cytology, computer science and mathematical modeling to understand the fundamental and emergent properties of neurons, glia and neural circuits.

I love it when science backs up the things we know or intuitively know to be true. Neuroscience has been helpful in connecting the dots as to how our brains process things and how everything works in a synergy that creates predictable results.

Recognizing that stressful events, adversities, and chronic circumstances can have big impacts on brain function, brain structure and can result in disorders, such as post-traumatic stress disorder (PTSD), depression, and other psychiatric issues, the field of neuroscience has committed substantial study into how the brain works, in experiencing stress and adversity, responding or adapting to it, and being what we have come to call: *resilient.*

While studies have shown that resilience does not activate one single area of the brain, they have found the most active area it relates to is the left prefrontal cortex of the brain. Neuroscience has sought to study what makes the brain function better and thus what makes an individual more resilient, as well as how resilience subsequently influences brain health and development.

There are several ways in which our brain functions to allow us to be resilient. One of those is perception or cognition, another is brain chemistry, and then there is neuroplasticity. The "plasticity" of the brain was first applied by William James in 1890 and was first used regarding neural function by the Polish Neuroscientist, Jerzy Konorski. Neuroplasticity is defined by Wikipedia as:

> also known as neural plasticity, or brain plasticity, is the ability of neural networks in the brain to change through growth and reorganization. These changes range from individual neuron pathways making new connections, to systematic adjustments like cortical remapping.

Neuroplasticity allows us to basically rewire our brains, forming new pathways, patterns and behaviors in response to the stimuli of stressors and adversity. These pathways form habits and strengths that become our patterned, subconscious responses. These will generally be repeated in the future when similar stimuli or circumstances are encountered.

The chemical aspects of brain function or dysfunction are well-known and long-studied, but the impact they have can play a strong part in our ability to be resilient and maintain it. When we understand both how brain chemicals affect our brain functions and how we stimulate the brain to produce or reduce these chemicals, we have valuable knowledge that is helpful in being and staying more in control and resilient.

The brain chemicals, known as neural transmitters, are complex and there is still a lot to learn about them; but we do know how they function regarding mood and emotions and subsequently, behaviors. There are actually hundreds of neurotransmitters and hormones that are flowing about between cells in our brains, and we are going to talk about a few of them right here.

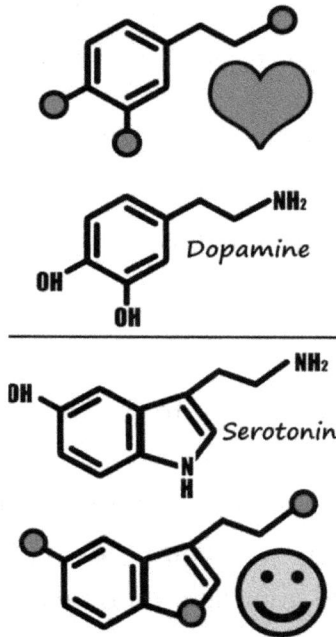

Our brains and bodies need dopamine, serotonin, oxytocin, and endorphins to function. Dopamine helps our brains categorize experiences as either important or pleasurable.

- **Serotonin** helps you to feel calm, confident, and balanced.
- **Oxytocin** aids in social bonding and intimacy. It is sometimes called the "cuddle hormone."

- **Endorphins** help to reduce pain and boost pleasure.
- **Cortisol** is also a brain chemical that is a stress alert for the body. It is known as the body's alarm system. It works with the body to control mood, motivation, and fear. While it is important to have this signaling hormone, too much of it causes stress and anxiety.

We have already talked a little about *perception,* or the cognitive aspect of brain function, and how that affects behavior. When you combine these three aspects of brain function it becomes apparent why neuroscience has become such a game-changer in the study of resilience, of why some people are more or less resilient, and how *joyful resilience* can work to help us in:

- Being more resilient
- Learning and teaching resilience
- Sustaining or maintaining a stronger core of resilience

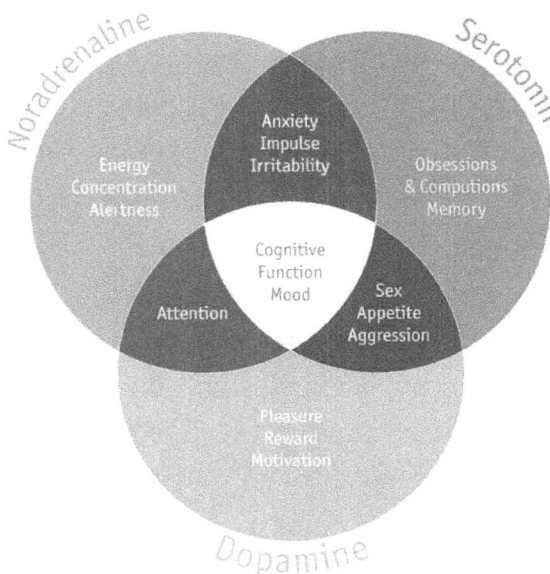

I will close this chapter with one additional thought about resilience that delving into all these studies on resilience has brought up for me. With a background in behavioral psychology, I am aware of the parameters that must be set for any area of research and study, and the limitations inherent in doing studies that really get to the bottom of how things work. The study of resilience, its interaction with joy or joyfulness, and what makes people more or less resilient is dually complex. This is one of the reasons information often takes a very long time to become commonplace or accepted; it necessarily includes numerous studies and input from multiple fields, as well as challenges and controversy.

A Note of Hope

I feel that some of the studies ignore the uniqueness of human experience and often define a person as "not being resilient" when they are actually going through a transformative and resilience-building experience. As a coach and hypnotherapist, I see people when they are feeling broken and defeated; seeing themselves as vulnerable and lacking resources. When I hear their stories though, I see they have usually had a long history of surviving and overcoming adversity, and have many resilience traits and experiences to draw upon. They just need a little tweak in perception and mindset, and sometimes a few tools to set them back on track. They have not stopped being resilient or lost anything, and they are not broken or even at a breaking point; they are just at a transition point in their resilience journey.

Chapter Four

What Are the Traits of Resilience?

"Life doesn't get easier or more forgiving, we get stronger and more resilient."

– Steve Maraboli

Resilience is not something we have or don't have, and it is not a "constant." It is a quality, a skillset or a toolbox, and survival mechanism. It is a primary response system that is made up of many traits that are constantly changing and evolving. When studies were done on resilience to see where it resides in the brain, nothing showed up. This is probably because it is not a single response, but more of a system of cells working in conjunction with one another. It is not merely determination, perseverance, or problem-solving skills that make a person resilient, but a combination of traits working together.

A person does not have to have all of the traits that contribute to resilience to be resilient, but having more of the traits and developing them more fully does make you more resilient. Below is a list of the traits that I have found help us to function more resiliently and definitions of those traits:

- Perception / awareness and insight – Knowledge about yourself and how you see the world around you
- Resourcefulness – Ability to draw upon internal and external sources for help or solutions
- Problem solving – Ability to look at a problem or issue from many perspectives to find answers
- Perseverance – Ability to stay on course and keep moving forward
- Confidence / self-esteem – Belief in yourself and your capabilities
- Adaptability – Ability to be flexible and bend to circumstances
- Hope – Expectations that things will happen for the best outcome
- Optimism – An outlook that sees the bright side or upside of things
- Creativity – Use of the imagination and innovation of new or original ideas
- Self-control, autonomy / locus of control – Ability to regulate one's own behavior, especially emotions, self-expression, and behavior
- Calmness – The state or quality of being free of anxiety, stress, or drama
- Determination – Resoluteness, steadfastness, firmness of purpose and intention

- Empathy – Ability to understand and share the feelings of others
- Sense of Humor – Ability to see humor in circumstances and occurrences
- Forgiveness – Ability to let go of negative feelings or emotions
- Compassion – Understanding and feeling empathy for the misgivings of self and others
- Gratitude – Appreciating and being thankful
- Faith / belief – Trust or confidence in someone or something
- Support / community – Other people to help us in times of need
- Self-love – Seeing, accepting, appreciating, and caring for yourself

The more of these traits you possess and the more highly developed they are, the more resilient you will be. All the above traits can be learned, nurtured, and further developed making it possible to continuously increase our responsiveness to adversity. We can also learn to access and draw upon these traits in times of difficulty and use them more effectively. When you add the powerful component of joyfulness to the above traits in any combination you become much more resilient.

What is Joyfulness?

It has been described as a state of being or condition of extreme well-being and good spirits. It is blessedness, bliss, cheer, gladness, happiness, felicity. It is the practice of joy as a core value, of embracing a state of contentment and peace as a destination to which you consistently return, or it is your home state of being. It is a state of extreme happiness, pleasure, awe, and wonderment.

Joy is defined as an internal feeling, whereas happiness is more of an outward expression of exuberance. Joy is an enduring state, while happiness can be momentary. Joy connects to deeper life meanings, such as purpose or passion, while happiness can be fleeting and temporary.

In accordance with the principles of neuroscience and positive psychology, when we are in a state of joyfulness our brains are functioning at an optimal level, and therefore we can be more resilient. How can we maintain or return to a state of joyfulness on a regular basis and form better habits and patterns to rewire our brains for both more resilience and more joyfulness? Here are some suggestions:

- Take care of your physical health. Body and brain are integrated.
- Smile. You may be amazed how much this affects your brain, body, and mood.
- Drink water. This affects body and brain function.
- Be present and mindful! Live in this moment.
- Slow down and allow yourself time for rest.
- Keep moving and exercise on a regular basis.
- Take breaks and breathe.
- Write down your feelings and get some perspective.
- Listen attentively and understand more.
- Take action on your goals.

- Schedule time for yourself.
- Celebrate the small wins along the way.
- Be optimistic or positive. Expect the best outcomes.
- Breathe. Pause for a breath. Practice breath control.
- Reduce and manage stress. Stop worrying!
- Music. Listen! Sing! Dance!
- Avoid and shift away from negativity.
- Laugh and look for the humor.
- Get enough sleep. This heals and restores body and brain.
- Have a plan for your day, week, and future goals.

Cultivating Resilience Traits

Resilience is much like a muscle and can be cultivated and strengthened in similar ways. It is developed through experience and made stronger and further defined with practice. When we go through adversity and overcome obstacles, we develop better responses for resilience. We can also develop the requisite skills and traits of resilience through different types of practices and disciplines.

For instance, meditation and mindfulness help us develop focus and clarity, which makes us more resilient. Solving math problems, putting together puzzles, or finding our way through a maze are all practices that help to develop our problem-solving and resourcefulness traits. For all the traits listed in this chapter, there are things you can do and things you do as part of your daily life that help to develop those traits and your readiness to be resilient in the face of adversity or difficult times.

Many models of resilience traits only include five to seven of the traits listed. However, I feel that all twenty are contributory to being our most resilient selves. Some researchers break down the traits into different categories of physical, mental, emotional, and psychological resilience. However, in a practical sense, they are all integrated into our functioning as resilient human beings. If you are a marathon runner you need to be physically resilient. However, physical resilience by itself is not enough. You must also be mentally and emotionally resilient to achieve your goals and push yourself to the highest levels of performance. There seem to be a few traits that really stand out in resilient individuals and seem to be more essential in getting through adversity. I call these "resilience superpowers."

Resilience Superpowers

The traits that seem to be overarching and particularly essential for resilience are the seven traits below. If you have these seven traits, you are likely getting through most of what life may throw your way.

- Self-Awareness / perception
- Adaptability – Ablility to bend and grow
- Staying calm and managing stress
- Empathy
- Self-control or locus of control
- Optimism
- Motivation, drive or perseverance

Why do I single these traits out as essential to being resilient? They are foundational for many of the other traits listed. Without these traits, you will have difficulty navigating adversity and developing or accessing many of the other traits and skillsets. Many of the other traits are important to resilience and will help immensely, but if you do not have empathy, you will not be able to cultivate forgiveness or compassion. If you do not have optimism, it is hard to feel hope. If you do not have self-control or a locus of control, it is hard to have determination, confidence, or resourcefulness and your problem-solving skills will be diminished.

When you have these seven "superpower" resilience traits and you add a core mindset of joyfulness, you have a formula for successfully navigating life's obstacles. It relates to the neuroscience of why "joy" enhances these traits. Our overall response to adversity is much stronger when we have joy. It's a fundamental part of how we are designed.

Nurturing your resilience superpowers is like making your car run better, last longer, and perform better when you need it to. You must maintain it, take care of it, and give it the right combination of ingredients for the engine and operating system to perform at their optimal level.

When we feel joyful, the neurotransmitters released into our bodies not only give us a euphoric, good feeling that we like, but those neurotransmitters reduce stress and make our immune systems stronger as well. We even have more physical strength when in a state of joy and all our brain circuitry works more quickly and efficiently. The brain on joy basically becomes a high-performance system. Of course, we will be more functional in dealing with life and its up and downs when in this state.

Chapter Five

"Only those who dare to fail greatly, can ever achieve greatly."

– Robert F. Kennedy

What is the History of Resilience?

Most of the articles and studies that mention resilience talk about the history of research and study in this area and how it has evolved. I discussed that to some degree in Chapter Three, dissecting how resilience is learned and taught. That is not what I want to talk about here regarding the history of resilience.

Rather, I want to discuss how our attitudes towards what we call resilience have developed and changed over time; how we've evolved over time in our ability to prevail. Since the beginning of time, we have had the capacity to respond to, react to, and essentially "deal with" adversity, even before we defined the response as resilience. With progressing studies, our definition of the characteristics and components of resilience has changed and evolved. This is what I want to talk about because it is very relevant to why *joyful resilience* is a wiser choice for us in modern resilience development.

Our thoughts and feelings are developed subconsciously; we adopt attitudes, habits, and beliefs through exposure to our environments, often without fully understanding why we feel what we do. Due to this subconscious or "automatic" adoption of beliefs, habits, and behaviors without conscious awareness; trauma and generational dysfunction perpetuate for decades, or even centuries, which are usually difficult to release, unlearn, and consciously recognize. Often, that which hurts us emotionally is beyond our awareness. In fact, even while still in the womb, we absorb messages, thoughts, feelings, and emotions from our mothers. We have the DNA of our grandmothers in our bodies. And so, we aren't really born with a blank slate...

We are born with some of the past, including some of the traumas, feelings, beliefs, fears, knowledge of our parents and generations past, already factory installed. What we believe, perceive, and feel is strongly affected by what has been accepted as truth and reality in the past. Change, letting go, and moving past these established norms is slow to happen. In order for our species to evolve and become more resilient, change, letting go, and moving past established norms is critical.

An ever-evolving human experience is challenging so learning the traits to survive has been hard-wired. We've evolved with certain beliefs needed to survive and thrive in our mental, physical, and emotional capacities. Our species has summarily taken to teaching and nurturing these beliefs from one generation to the next. You have probably heard the response, "I don't know, we've always done it that way," at some point, in response to asking the question: "why?"

If we look back centuries on the lives of humankind, we see that existence has been pretty challenging, especially in the very beginning, where a large percentage of life was simply focused on survival. Our first ancestors spent most of their time finding food and shelter while trying to avoid becoming prey to various predators. They had limited tools and resources to help them in this struggle. Therefore, the attitude and mindset we developed had to be focused on this hard, survival-based life. If you are being chased by a saber-toothed tiger and must not only hunt, kill, clean and cook your dinner over an open flame that must be started by rubbing rocks together and water that's only available at the riverside, your life is hard, and its focus is limited and austere by necessity.

What, historically, do we or have we believed about resilience or the ability to meet, rise above, and bounce back after adversity? Physically, we must be strong and fast. Emotionally, we must be tough, persistent, and focused. Mentally, we must be adaptable, agile, and resourceful. All these things are true, but what did they mean back thousands of years ago and what do they mean now?

Finding meaning or codes of behavior that lead to the needed qualities for surviving, thriving, and bouncing back from adversity or being resilient has been a big part of how our attitudes have formed.

If you look at history and the formation of laws, rules, and religious belief systems, they have been focused on creating behaviors within society appropriate for the times that would lead to the greatest chances for surviving and thriving. This is how it was originally. As time has passed, many survival mechanisms in our brains have been continued which are no longer necessary in our current times. Attitudes and beliefs are often slower to evolve and change than life circumstances, and that is certainly true in the fast-changing world we have been living in for at least the last few centuries. We are still hanging on to some attitudes and beliefs that made sense back in the 1700s, but today don't serve our needs, best interests, awareness, and the goals of surviving and thriving in today's world.

From our hard survival history and some of the big adversities we faced over time, we developed some cultural and societal philosophies on living life, and some of them have not been updated to match the conditions of our lives, the resources available to us, and the learning we have gleaned over time.

Stoicism as a philosophy evolved in the 3rd century. It offered some good resources in the evolution of logical thinking, but also lead to some incorrect responses and unhealthy behaviors. Over time, as we developed more tools and resources for dealing with survival concerns, the focus of resilience changed and took on more characteristics of character, thought processes, social norms, and mores, rather than brute strength. This was taken up to a great extent by a focus on religious and philosophic ideas. Fundamentalism became a strong underpinning of our survival beliefs and the characteristics needed in Western culture beginning in the 19^(th) century, growing largely out of different religious philosophies. While life in the early 16^(th), 17^(th), 18^(th), and 19^(th) centuries was by no means easy, it was not solely focused on survival.

The transition from a solely survival-based society to one that left room for other pursuits led to some conflicting ideas on exactly what was needed and how people should or should not behave to survive, thrive and overcome adversity.

While in our modern times it is widely accepted that pleasure, enjoyment, fun, play, and happiness are not only acceptable, but desirable components of our daily lives, it was not that long ago that they were considered wrong, wasteful, harmful, or even sinful. It was believed well into the 19^(th) century that work was a virtue and all else would lead us astray. There was a nose-to-the-grindstone attitude that survived well after its time and there was no recognized value in the pursuit of anything that indulged our emotions or pursuit of pleasure. Those pursuits were largely thought to bring failure, loss, destruction, and poverty or, at worst, eternal damnation. Thus, they were discouraged and frowned upon. Suffering was often considered a virtue to be later rewarded.

We now know through study in several fields that those things that take us away from work, providing respite and uplifting us with pleasure and joy responses, make us stronger and more resilient in dealing with adversity and obstacles of all kinds. We have learned, of course, that it is a matter of balance, but a life without joy leaves us more vulnerable to all those things that can harm and devastate us, contrary to many past beliefs. This perception is now recognized, but many of those old beliefs still hang on in many people, in some religious and societal beliefs that are slow to change, and this is why sometimes people feel that they need to behave in ways and live their lives in ways that make them less resilient. They feel guilty about being joyful, that they must always be strong and suppress their emotions, or that they will fail if they stop to enjoy life, especially in times of loss and adversity.

This is the suffering and sadness model of resilience I mentioned in the beginning of the book. It is the "pull yourself up by the bootstraps, grind it out, toughen up and push yourself through things no matter what" attitude of resilience. It is not wrong, and people do get through adversity with this attitude and mindset, but it is hard, spirit-crushing, passion-killing resilience. It influences the way we see life, how our brains work, our health and well-being. It is a way of being resilient and rising above adversity, but it is not the only way, and it is not the best way in our modern times when we know better.

In Debbie Hampton's article, "Culture Shock Really is Brain Shock," she talks about some of the reasons why making these changes and adaptions takes time. They really are hard-wired in our brains. She says, "Not only does man's brain shape and make culture, but a person's culture shapes and makes their brain because of neuroplasticity, the ability of the brain to change form and function in response to repeated behaviors, emotions and thoughts."

Thus, the life you live and the culture you live in shape your brain, thoughts, and beliefs. And ultimately it is neuroplasticity that allows this to change and evolve over time.

Today, we can choose *joyful resilience* and yes, it is a choice. We can choose to make joy our core mindset and build our resilience or response to life and its adversities from that foundation.

We have abundant tools and resources to help us in forming the mindset and traits that will help us when life throws us those evitable curve balls that bring us to our knees and leave us devastated.

"Turn Your wounds into wisdom."

- Oprah Winfrey

Chapter Six

"Challenges are gifts that force us to search for a new center of gravity.Don't fight them. Just find a new way to stand."

– Oprah Winfrey

Clearing Limiting Beliefs & Energy Blocks

If our past, both as individuals and as a society, has left us with the baggage of unconscious and subconscious beliefs, thoughts, and feelings that stand in our way, keeps us from functioning optimally, or blocks us from moving past adversities and obstacles that we encounter in life, how do we deal with this? It's not easy, but it is entirely possible and much needed. We must evolve, through a process of change and transformation and let go of those ideas, attitudes, beliefs, and behaviors that no longer serve us.

When beliefs have been shown by research, science, and other reliable methods to be untrue or dysfunctional, or have simply outlived their relevance to our lives and current times, it is necessary to dispose of them, throw them away, and replace them with better alternatives. It is a bit like cleaning out your closet, throwing away things that don't fit, that are outdated, that you haven't worn in years, don't really like or you shouldn't have bought in the first place. We do this with physical items in our lives and we need to do it with the mental and emotional clutter, as well.

Many of us procrastinate on or never do this mental and emotional clearing for many different reasons. A lot of people also procrastinate or never do the clearing of stuff in their physical world, but most of us reach a point where it becomes evident that it is necessary, and we just do it.

With the mental and emotional clutter, however, we often remain unaware of its existence and the problems they cause for longer periods of time because it is intangible or invisible and it doesn't pile up in such an obvious way. It does, however, keep building and eventually we reach a point where it hinders our functioning and creates obstacles to moving forward and dealing with life in the most efficient and optimal ways. As with physical clutter, we are forced to deal with it when we realize it is obstructing our pathway. This point is most often reached in the throes of adversity and devastation, when we are trying to deal with very difficult times and just feel like we are stuck and out of options for coping.

When we encounter these blocks in the roadway and feel there is no path forward, that is the time we must pivot and realize that something must change on a deep level within us. It is apparent that our roadmap and operating system are not working and we must look for guidance.

Most people have difficulty clearing the limiting beliefs and energy blocks in their lives because they are unaware of their existence and don't know where to start or how to do it.

Clearing Limiting Beliefs

The initial step to overcoming blocks and clearing limiting beliefs is recognizing where you are stuck and what is holding you back. When we feel stuck, there is usually a conflict going on inside of us. We are out of alignment in some way, parts of our belief system or thought processes are not fitting in and working in conjunction with the rest of our beliefs, thoughts, ideas, and attitudes.

We must identify what is not working and keeping us from being able to move forward and make decisions about how to proceed in the direction we need to go. It is not an easy process, as I stated earlier, because we must really examine all our thoughts and feelings to get to the source of those limiting beliefs that can be buried in layers of experience, some of which may not even be our own. Our parents pass many of their attitudes or beliefs on to us because of their learning and experience and we internalize much of it believing it to be true, even though we have not experienced it ourselves.

An example of this is my mother, who grew up very poor during the depression, where her mother raised five children working as a waitress, struggling to make ends meet. She told me many times about what that was like and emphasized the value of money and material things and, in particular, the need to take care of things on a constant basis. As a result, even though I always had more than enough growing up and never felt poor, I developed a habit of taking extremely good care of all my things so they would last a long time and was reluctant to throw anything away. It was well into adulthood before I realized that I had internalized my mother's fear of not having enough and was therefore hanging on to everything I had way beyond its normal life expectancy.

On one hand, this served me well, but in many cases, it did not; it led to me keeping a large amount of stuff that was very literally garbage that should have been long ago discarded. This is just one example of a limiting belief that needed to be recognized and cleared away, but we all have many, thus we need to examine and update our software, so to speak, on a regular basis. There are many areas and types of limiting beliefs for all of us, but dealing with them can be handled in similar ways, regardless of where we encounter them in our lives.

How do we go about clearing limiting beliefs? It is a process of changing our internal framework, the set of beliefs or truths that we have as the basis for our thought processes, behaviors, and perception of reality. We shift or change our perspective and look at things differently. There is a structure for this that has been found to be effective, but everyone will progress through this process in different ways on their own timetables. If you follow the process though, I believe it is possible for everybody to transform limiting beliefs into new perspectives and *joyful resilience*.

Here's how to start clearing your limiting beliefs:

- Identify a limiting belief. Find what is stopping you, holding you back, or causing fear.
- Recognize that it is just a belief and not a fact. Find the source of the belief.
- Challenge your own beliefs. Usually done by asking questions and finding evidence.
- Recognize the consequences of holding on to this belief.
- Adopt a new, more functional belief.
- Put the new belief into practice. Act on it and see how it works and feels.

While this may seem simple, when you take each step and go through the processes, you may find that it takes a fair amount of work, but it is extremely transformative. This is an effective and empowering process that you can use to change your life in ways you may not have imagined. Fundamentally, neuroscience confirms that identifying something you want to change, naming that thing you want to change, and creating a mental plan for new action is critical to the conscious rewiring of stuck, subconscious patterns.

Here is an example of clearing a limiting belief. I once had a client who was constantly bullied by his two older brothers. He was a grown adult in his sixties and still found it hard to stand up for himself and assert his own wants and needs. His brothers were the main people that he had trouble doing this with, but it also spilled over into other areas of his life and other relationships. He was aware of the problems, which caused him distress, but he did not know how to deal with them. He was very close to his brothers and valued the relationship they had.

First, we identified the reasons he felt he could not stand up to his brothers and express his feelings about things or express what his fears were:

- He was afraid they would get angry.
- He was afraid they would reject him, or it would ruin their close relationship.
- He was afraid they would not respect him or his desires.

We delved into why he believed these things would happen if he stood up for himself and asserted his own views and wishes. It went back a lot of years, and we did some hypnosis and NLP to help him with realizing that attitudes from childhood may not be relevant today.

Next, I asked him to have a conversation with his brothers about his new goal of being more assertive and ask them for their opinions, advice, and help in accomplishing this goal. It turns out that his brothers also saw his lack of assertiveness as a problem (although they did not see their role in it as clearly). Their intentions were good and they wanted to help him in this endeavor. They had reacted differently than he would have expected. His limiting beliefs and fear over trying to change this behavior turned out to be false; his brothers did not get angry;

they did not reject him, and it improved their relationship. He found that they respected him more and were happy to see him assert himself.

It took an action plan for being more assertive and some work on his part to keep acting on this goal, realizing that the consequences of not doing so were continued frustration and unhappiness, but it effectively helped my client build more confidence and a better sense of control over his entire life. Since this exercise involved interaction with his brothers, there were some setbacks and boundaries he needed to set, but with continued effort, he was able to see himself as more empowered and not feel bullied by his brothers.

Positive affirmations are strong tools for forming new mindsets and overcoming limiting beliefs; they are a favorite tool of NLP practitioners. Below are a few favorite general affirmations to add to your toolbox. I will talk more about why and how affirmations work later in this book.

1. I start my day with a peaceful mind and a grateful heart.
2. I welcome and expect blessings and abundance into my life.
3. Everything will work out for the best.
4. I am open and allow all the love I deserve into my life.
5. I always have enough and attract abundance to me.
6. I am deserving, worthy, loved, and enough.
7. I have unlimited imagination and ideas.

Give these a try by simply repeating them on a regular basis and see how it works. You may want to write them down and have them on your bathroom mirror or above your desk. As you repeat these affirmations daily, I suspect you'll be quickly surprised at their effectiveness for uplifting your overall spirit and mindset throughout your day.

There are many tools and techniques for clearing limiting beliefs with hypnosis, NLP, EFT, visualization, and manifesting all being very effective and commonly used. You can visit me at

https://www.soulfirewisdom.com/contact/ or scan this link to schedule your Soul Fire Wisdom session with me to develop your own blueprint for freedom from limiting beliefs.

Clearing Energy Blocks

While all limiting beliefs create energy blocks, not all energy blocks are caused by limiting beliefs. There are other types of things that block the flow of energy in our bodies and cause us to remain stuck and unable to move forward. We are energetic beings and everything is energy. Everything needs to flow freely, much like an electrical circuit, for us to function optimally, as we are naturally meant to. Like an electrical circuit, if there is a blockage or something diminishing the flow, something that disrupts the flow or disconnects the circuits, we will remain stuck or become completely dysfunctional, and stop working altogether. There are several different types of energy blocks that commonly leave us feeling stuck.

We experience these energy blocks in different ways in our bodies. Common symptoms of energy blocks are low energy, illness, pain, mental fog, aches, headache, anxiety, anger, and unexplained fear. The sources of these blockages can be varied. Energy psychology and energy research are fairly new fields of study with very old roots, and there is a lot to them. Some areas intersect with neuroscience and positive psychology and some rely on the sciences of biology, physics, chemistry, and even engineering. Another part of it has a lot of what is still considered by many as "woo," wonder, or magic because it is not based on concrete studies, but on thousands of years of knowledge, lore, intuitive messages, and such.

Here I am going to try to give some very simple explanations that will make the way things work understandable on the broadest level, leaving out much of the history, language, and specific fields of study that make up the ongoing studies in this emerging field. I am going to break it down to flow. When I talk about clearing energy blocks, I am talking about clearing away blockages to the flow of all life forces that keep us stuck and unable to move forward mentally, emotionally, physically, or spiritually.

Aside from limiting beliefs, several other types of blockages keep us stuck. These are:

- Suppressed emotions or trauma.

- Denying or being out of alignment with your true self.
- Disregarding or putting yourself and your needs last.
- Letting challenges define you (such as illness, injury, disability, or circumstance).
- Allowing other people's energy to overwhelm or dominate you.

Any of these will cause you to be stuck in thinking and patterns that block, disrupt, or disconnect you from the flow of life and keep you stuck in dysfunction. All of these things can be worked through and resolved, and energy clearing is an effective way of aiding in that process to restore our life flow. Below are some ways of clearing or healing energy blocks:

- Do a cleanse or detox
- Have a reiki session or learn the practice of reiki
- Mediation
- Eat a healthy clean diet
- Get lots of sunlight
- Practice feng shui
- Practice yoga, tai chi or qigong
- Unplug (disconnect from devices, social media, news, etc.}
- Breathing exercises
- Create / shift mindset
- Practice mindfulness
- Personal rituals – burning sage, essential oils, chakra clearing, etc.

All the above suggestions will help you to do the internal work of clearing away those emotional and mental blocks that are impeding the flow of your life energies and keeping you stuck. This is important to both resilience and joyful resilience, and for being our most joyful and resilient selves since we must be functioning well and have all our lifeforce energy flowing optimally.

There still is a lot of study to be done in the energy field and much to learn to really understand how important energy is and the intricacies of how it all works. One thing we do know is that literally everything is energy! You will find a free gift of an "Energy Clearing, Healing and Awakening Reiki Mediation" in the final chapter. Be sure to download and listen whenever you need it. It is great for starting your day or balancing when you are feeling anxious or stressed.

> *"Our beliefs shape our experience. If we can let go of what we know, we'll put ourselves on a path with new possibilities."*
>
> – Jeanne McElvaney, Light in the Shadows

Part Two

Resilience Stories – The Inspiration

In Chapters Seven through Eleven, I share stories of resilience that will motivate and inspire the reader. You may see yourself and something from your own resilience journey in the stories or you may see resilience beyond anything you have experienced. You will see many of the traits that make up resilience in the stories. There are my own stories, the stories of friends and stories of 10 contributing authors to motivate and inspire you. I hope you will see the part that joy played and the role it has in making us stronger and more resilient

Chapter Seven

"If your heart is broken make art with the pieces."

– Shane Koyczan

My Stories: Learning Resilience

This book on resilience was always on my list, but writing it first was not and it was definitely the pandemic and our year-plus of COVID-19 that led me to write the book now, rather than later. It is also relevant that I moved to Southern Arizona, with its desert climate, during this time and all around me there were examples of extraordinary resilience.. If one were looking for signs, it would seem that I was definitely presented with them in abundance.

I am blessed to have strong experience and education in the area of resilience. I have been gifted to have learned from my family, my own experience, and the experience of others including close friends and clients through my work. I am continually educated by the resilience experiences of my clients, who further educate me daily by bringing stories I would never otherwise imagine. In my job as a hypnotherapist and life coach, I help clients often when everything else has failed. I like to call myself a change adventure navigator. As a guide, I lead clients to find their way through obstacles and adversity. In the process, I am continually gifted with the stories clients confide and trust me with and the learning I am honored to gain from them. Here is is a quote from my website.

> *"I feel so honored and blessed to be able to help people in this way. I am grateful for the trust they place in me and I am always in awe of the strength and joy they find within. Life can be really difficult and sometimes unfair. The human spirit, however, never fails to hold me in complete amazement. Some of my clients come to me feeling broken and defeated. It is my greatest pleasure to show them how brave, courageous, and truly resourceful they really are. What I love most about what I do is when I see someone not only feeling joyful and confident in the present moment, but knowing they will be okay and have the tools they need no matter what the future may bring. I love to see people living with purpose and passion sharing their unique gifts."*

> – Kate Olson

I am sharing here some stories from my own life that taught me about resilience and led me to joyful resilience, enlightening me on my own evolving journey.

Mom's Broken Heart

My mother was the strongest person I have ever known to this day. She passed away at sixty-two, of massive heart failure. Even though she had been sick most of my life, it was still both a surprise and a shock that she died suddenly. It was a difficult loss, compounded by my father's unexpected death just two months later. She was the second oldest of five children and the oldest daughter. She grew up in North Dakota. After a long illness, her father died when she was eleven. Her mom raised the kids mostly on her own working as a waitress at the only steak house in a small town. My mom took care of her siblings. They did not have an easy life. They struggled through the depression. I remember her telling me that they ate lard and sugar sandwiches. My grandmother remarried, but her second husband got sick too, so again she was the caretaker. They were poor. My mom talked about only having two dresses and being bullied at school. At sixteen, she was diagnosed with rheumatic fever, missed a long period of school, and ended up dropping out. She wanted to be a nurse and probably would have pursued that course if she had not gotten sick. She went to work full-time and started dating a shy, popular boy whose family was more affluent and owned a business in town. That was my father. He was a kind and affable man but suffered from social anxiety, which he self-medicated with alcohol. I was born when my mom was twenty. It was a difficult birth and my mom was told she couldn't have more children.

Motherhood was hard on her. She was always exhausted and anxious, but it wasn't until she was thirty-two that she was diagnosed with a heart condition caused by her rheumatic fever. My sister was six then and I was pretty much her caretaker or second mom, as my mother was not doing well. The valve carrying blood to her heart was the size of a thread and it was supposed to be the size of your thumb. When she was diagnosed, the cardiologist told her that she was literally a few months from death if she didn't have surgery. Her skin was gray, she had no energy, yet was always anxious. My mom was a bit obsessive-compulsive and her go-to when she felt bad was to clean. Our house was spotless and you literally couldn't walk on her beautiful hardwood floors without Mom having an anxiety attack. She needed open heart surgery and they were not sure she would make it. She was actually one of the first open-heart surgeries and it was a very complicated surgery at the time. She made it though, and it was like she came back to life. There was a long recovery period, but from right after the surgery you could see the color come back into her skin and the hope come back to her eyes. I did not really realize how close we'd come to losing her until I saw the signs of life returning in her. All of my life she been slowly dying, becoming more angry, and even more mentally unwell. She went through a process of transformation that really made her celebrate the value of life. She actually seemed happy and joyful for the first time. As long as I had known her, she had been overwhelmed and unhappy with only moments of joy that were very fleeting and short-lived. My dad's drinking had increased with the stress of her illness and, even though he loved her and had good intentions, he could not be the support she needed. She turned to distractions for solace. I won"t go into any details here, but my parent's relationship deteriorated. My dad's alcoholism got worse and, eventually, they got a divorce. Mom wanted more of a relationship and actually began a new relationship before their divorce was final, with the man who later became my step-father. I saw her embrace life for about sixteen years. They were not planning it, but my half-brother was born when she was thirty-nine and he became the child she could actually raise and be herself with, for a time. I really had to get to know my mom again, as she definitely was not the same person who had raised me. Unfortunately, all of the issues caused by her rheumatic fever had not been discovered and new symptoms started to appear over time. She got a rare form of arthritis and her heart issues were not fully resolved. They did not discover it until after her death, but the rheumatic fever had caused small perforations in her heart that ultimately led to her death. She struggled the last years of her life with debilitating illness, but she kept going and really did not want to let go of life.

The way she lived the last years of her life was such a contrast to the early years, I saw growing up. Growing up I saw an angry, bitter, and impatient woman with a short temper. She took her rage out on the world and more specifically, on my father and me. Though my dad was an alcoholic and drank, in part pushed by the stress he felt, he was an adult and did understand what she was going through. I wanted to understand, but I was just a child and it was more difficult. I remember once asking my dad why Mom hated me and he said she didn't. He told me, "You just have to understand your mom." That was hard for a child when she would strike out for no reason and hit, yell or say horrible things. It was hard to know that the rage was not really directed at me when it definitely felt that way. On some level, I did get the message that she loved me and there was something going on with her, but it took many years of resentment and hurt to heal the wounds. This was another pain for my mother as well, as she did not know how to heal the distance growing between us and it hurt her too. Once she had learned to be joyful, she wasn't willing to let go of it. I believe that finding joy and happiness prolonged her life and made the quality of her life better despite the illness and pain she suffered. I also believe that the many earlier years of her illness with the pain, anger, and bitterness she felt took their toll and contributed to her later illness and early death. I wish that she had not had to endure the long years of suffering not knowing what was wrong, but I learned so much from her experience. A letter she wrote me six months before she passed helped me acknowledge that she had learned as much as I had and understood the journey she had gone through. She had been enlightened in many similar ways. That provided a lot of healing to our relationship. That letter would be a necessary key in my own later journey and healing. Though I don't have the letter anymore, it still gives me great comfort. I see my mom's heart much like the Japanese art of Kintsugi, where broken pieces are mended to create both greater strength and a different beauty, a magnificent symbol of resilience.

Learning Hard Lessons

I witnessed and was a part of my mother's story and, on some level, I knew that suffering, anger, and bitterness were not emotions that we should hold on to, but still, this is what I saw and this is what I did. I felt and believed I was unloved and unlovable. I was everyone's friend, except my own and as a co-dependent, I was looking for someone to fill me up and make it better. I was extremely insecure and had no idea how to have a healthy relationship. I got married, had a son and then, suddenly, my marriage fell apart. It seemed like suddenly, but actually, it had been building and I had just ignored the signs. Someone I counted on betrayed me, well not just one someone, but two people I loved and trusted, betrayed me. I fell apart and felt devastated, and at first, I didn't acknowledge it. I stumbled, ignored, and played the victim for years until I worked myself to a complete crisis point. I was empty, depleted, and had no self-reservoir to draw upon. I suffered from PTSD both from childhood trauma and the undealt with trauma of loss from my divorce. I was never a big drinker but had the propensity for addiction and co-dependence with an alcoholic father and grandfather. For me, the addiction I ended up falling prey to, was gambling; I enjoyed playing blackjack. The idea there was logic to it, rather than just luck appealed to me. There was an element of hope and possibility to it as well, and I was actually good at it. Of course, logically I knew it wasn't good for me, it was purely an emotional distraction. However, like all distractions and in accordance with addict behavior, that did not deter me from doing it. I played enough to lose a job and lost enough money to get evicted and have to send my son to live with his dad for his last year of high school. That was really devastating for me emotionally. I truly felt like a total failure. Being a good and supportive mom was something that was important to me, and I felt I had done pretty well. Although my son looks back at it as a needed lesson, I still wonder how his life would have been different, if it had not happened. It was a perfect distraction that validated my lack of self-esteem. I truly did hit rock bottom before realizing I was in a place I didn't want to be. It made me take a hard look and realize I was the only person who could do something about it. It took me more than a few stumbles and a lot of self-awareness, examination, and a bit of forgiveness to do that. There were some contributing factors that added to my distress. I had a long-term stalker, who caused havoc in my life at the worst times and I was afraid to confront it head-on for many reasons, including my low self-esteem, for many years. There were also a couple of cases of workplace harassment that added both to my stress and financial instability. Though somewhat out of my control, ignoring these situations and refusing to confront them both confirmed my victim status and made me feel even more stuck. There were also ongoing health issues that really began when my son was born. During pregnancy, thyroid issues had shown up and the doctor told me it was common and usually temporary. Over the following years, I was generally sick a lot with a myriad of symptoms and they never pinned down any cause. This led me to feel frustrated and guilty because I just wasn't up to dealing with life. It was twelve years before they diagnosed my thyroid issues and Hashimoto's disease. It was another ten years before I dealt with all the issues, including severe digestive issues and weight gain, and got my health really in balance. And then there were two really serious accidents; one car accident that involved surgery, a year of physical therapy, a pin and plate that are still in my ankle; and the other a fall where I broke my elbow for the second time. This second break pretty much shattered my elbow and they put it back together with three good-sized screws. It took a good year and a half to get back to functional and I don't quite have full movement, although I can do almost everything. I used to say, "If it wasn't for bad luck, I would have no luck at all." I really felt that way and felt that I had little control over what was happening in my life. This puzzled me on one level and also the people that had known me growing up, like my sister and some long-time friends, as I had been very much a resilient, take-control, high achiever growing up. I was the one that didn't have problems, for the most part, and always helped others. I was the "good girl."

Finally, I did realize I was creating my own dilemmas and needed to take another course. I pretty much had no options at that time. I was sleeping on a friend's sofa a few nights a week and living in my car the other nights, when my car broke down in the middle of a busy intersection. I had to call my sister and brother-in-law to ask for help. I wasn't in contact with them at the time, so it was definitely hard. I had lived in my sister's basement for a while, but she and I had had a big argument,t so I had moved out with no place to go. I had to let go of my ego and mend that bridge. It was both difficult and healing. I lived in my sister's basement again for a year, got a job, bought a real junker car, and slowly started rebuilding. I slowly made small changes, starting with my actions, then with attitudes, moving to habits, and finally to who I was or who I saw myself becoming. I remember my sister telling me I wasn't myself and thinking, of course I wasn't, but I really did not know how to find myself again. It took me a full five years from when I was evicted from my apartment to get back to living in an apartment that I shared with my son for three years. Finally, I moved to my own apartment and, for the first time in my life, had a place of my own, all alone. That was a big adjustment and very empowering for me at the time. The steps to rebuilding began first with long walks and reflection, then forgiveness, both of others and myself. When I was able to start giving again and helping others, that was when my life really took a big leap forward. The final step, where I really found myself, was going back and getting reacquainted with myself as a girl growing up. She was a strong, resilient girl who found the good and joy in everything. I remembered once being her and slowly I found her still there inside me. I really liked that girl; she was a somewhat precocious and amazing little person. Integrating the current me and all that I had learned and become with that core me was the beginning of a new life. I remembered how my mom had changed and I knew I was capable too, of becoming a better and more genuine version of myself. Like her, I knew that my life was not about what had happened to me and I deserved something better. As I added more joy and gratitude to my life, as I forgave and worked on making positive changes, I was amazed at how my life, my circumstances, my outlook, and my aspirations all changed immensely and fairly quickly. I came alive again too and I am still living happily in joyful resilience, despite whatever life might bring my way, including the chaos and adversity of 2020. I am happy, joyful, and grateful for the beautiful life I continue to create day by day, moment by moment. My experience is not one I would recommend as far as the adversities I went through, but it was an invaluable lesson and I am so grateful to have learned from it. It has made me who I am and I so love her and the life I am creating. I know there will be obstacles and adversity to come, maybe worse than those I've seen so far, but I also know I will deal with them and I will live with joy as long as I have the privilege of doing so. I am blessed, grateful, and joyful to the core of my being.

Gifts Learned from Rejection & Exclusion

This is something we have all confronted and still it is one of the hardest and most commonly traumatizing experiences we go through. Most of us learn to deal with it and get past it, but some never do and the results can be quite devastating. I am called to write about this for two reasons: I have recently been confronted with the remnants of a trauma created by feelings of rejection and also, a client recently told me about a family members' inability to deal with emotional trauma, and subsequent suicide, after feeling rejected and excluded by those she wanted to feel accepted by. This is, of course, is an extreme and heart-breaking outcome, but I am guessing there are very few people who cannot relate to the emotional pain that rejection and exclusion can cause. These feelings can be quite crushing and there is almost no one who has not felt them. The question is; how do people learn to cope with and get past these feelings, to move forward and take the gifts of resilience to make them stronger the next time around?

Acceptance and validation are quite basic to our needs and very few of us get enough of these to build our self-worth, self-love, and resilience to a level of confidence where we are truly secure and rejection-proof. At least, we seldom get it in childhood and not without a lot of introspection, awareness, and self-esteem-building work. Most of us are raised by adults who have not yet attained this level of self-worth themselves and don't know how to give it to us. Additionally, we face a world that bombards us with self-esteem diminishing challenges on a regular basis. It seems to be the nature of humans to try to build their own self-worth at the expense of others when they don't know more healthy ways of doing so. We see it all around us and it is modeled for us in some cases. It is possible, though, to grow and become stronger from these experiences.

From childhood into adulthood, we see it. Two friends make themselves feel superior by talking about what they see as a shortcoming in someone else. Or in today's world, one group of people criticizes and villainizes another group of people over beliefs and ideologies. Many times, we don't think this is a big deal until we are on the receiving side. The people that are bonding and feeling superior, often lack any empathy for the feelings of the person they are diminishing. That is sometimes because they do not really know the person and sometimes because they do and want to purposefully exclude or diminish them for their own benefit.

I am going to share a story from my own childhood that had a huge impact on me in so many ways. While today I consider it a blessing, as the feelings I experienced give me a special empathy to advocate for helping people to feel confident and resilient, at the time it was difficult. I was always a fairly kind and inclusive child with a strong sense of fairness, so excluding others or making them feel bad was never something I did. Pretty much the opposite was true. It was really my philosophy to be kind, inclusive, and help others if I could.

In fourth grade, a classmate had a bird that she brought to school and that bird became the class pet. She was very attached to her bird, as most of us are to our pets. She shared the bird with the class though and allowed others to care for it. Over one weekend, something happened and the bird died. The whole class felt bad and mourned the loss, but it was really hard on the owner of the bird. I had empathy and felt very sad for her. I had an idea of getting her another bird and instead of doing it myself, I organized a group of her other friends and we all planned together to raise the money, get the bird, and give it to her. I thought everything was going quite well. I was excited that we were going to be able to do this as a group and hopefully help our friend feel better.

I had no idea that there were any problems brewing in the group. I had known most of the girls for years and felt they were my friends. One day, just a few days before we were going to give the bird to our mutual friend, one of girls asked me to meet her down on the baseball field after school. I didn't really think much about it and went to meet her, seeing that the rest of our group was there too. Still, I thought nothing of it. I had never been bullied or had enemies, for the most part, so nothing occurred to me. Suddenly, the group formed a circle around me and skipped in a circular motion while chanting, "We vote you out!" I was taken completely off guard and it took a few minutes to even figure out what they were doing and what it meant. And then, one of them explained that they were excluding me from the group and I would not be allowed to participate in the plans for giving the bird to our friend. I was just out! My stomach felt like it dropped to my feet and I simply couldn't speak. I was hurt more than I could have expressed and no words would come out of my mouth. I looked at them trying not to let myself cry and then I walked away as fast as I could. When I got out of their sight, I ran all the way home before I cried. The feeling was horrific and I had no idea why they had done this. I also did not know how to deal with it or my feelings. I had a hard time going to school the next day and couldn't look at any of the girls. It hurt that my friend did not know that her new bird had been from me as well as the other girls and that it had been my idea, but I didn't say anything. After what seemed like months, but it was really only days, some of the girls in the group started coming and apologizing to me, telling me that one of the girls had instigated what had happened by telling the rest of them that I was too bossy and didn't deserve to be in the group. She was jealous and wanted to be in charge of things. Sadly, she didn't know that I wasn't really set on being the boss and would have let her have more say if she had spoken up rather than tossing me aside. Eventually, all the girls except the instigator apologized to me and even the girl who received the bird told me she had been told it had been my idea. That helped, but the feelings and mistrust hung on much longer. I avoided the girl who instigated things for the rest of the time we were in school together, even though we had been friends. I am not sure if she knew that I knew about what she had done. She still talked to me and acted friendly from time to time. I had not realized before that how insecure and insincere she apparently was, but of course, I knew I couldn't trust her and didn't want to deal with her. I did forgive her. Though I never wanted to experience anything like that again, it strangely made me stronger, and getting through it gave me confidence. It would be decades, many more experiences, and much self-reflection and self-acceptance before I would feel confident enough to put that trauma behind me. It was the start of a very important lesson on dealing with rejection and exclusion. A lesson I am very thankful for, despite the pain involved. I gained a sort of "Spidey-Sense" for picking up the energy of those people who, due to their own needs, would be inclined to throw me under the bus, so to speak, and I have learned to opt-out or avoid them before they have the chance to do so. Usually without any malice. I have come to realize that they are doing the best they can with what they know.

I did encounter the instigator of that grade-school trauma again on a break after my first year of college. I went into a local store on a visit home and was looking around when I heard a voice excitedly call my name. When I turned around, the girl who had caused me that pain way back when had a big smile on her face. She grabbed me and hugged me, saying how happy she was to see me. I was in momentary shock as I recognized her and took everything in. She had surprisingly gained a good forty pounds and looked a bit different. We talked for a while and caught up on what we had been doing since high school. I was surprised to find out that she was on a break from college and working full-time at the store. She had dropped out of school during her freshman year after having an emotional breakdown. I listened to her story and empathized as she told me of her feelings of not fitting in, being excluded, and having trouble keeping up academically. She seemed to feel better as I empathized. I asked her about her future plans and encouraged her, reminding her of the skills and abilities I knew she had. There was that moment where I felt a twinge of revenge brewing, but I opted for compassion. She hugged me again before I left and said she was glad we bumped into each other and that I had always been a loyal and kind friend. I was happy in the end to know she thought of me that way. She went back to school the following fall at a college in the Midwest where she still lives. She graduated, married, had a beautiful family, and was doing well when I last heard. I did wonder if she ever thought about her actions and how they had affected me. I realized it really didn't matter, as it wouldn't have changed a thing. I was happy I had chosen to react with compassion and knew it was the better choice.

There are many types of rejection and exclusion, and they bombard us throughout life. Breakup, divorce, job loss, not getting the job, award, raise, praise, or accolades that we wanted, hoped for, or deserved. We do need to feel and process those emotions, no matter how painful. In the end, I took the lessons and moved forward, a little bruised, but so much stronger and wiser. The gifts far outweighed the rest. Pay attention to your intuition as much as you can and avoid people and situations that end up draining you or feel wrong and toxic. Rejection isn't always avoidable, but try not to take it personally. It likely isn't about you. Lastly, it is usually not fatal, although it can feel that way. If nothing else, it will give you strength and character, even when that doesn't seem possible at the time. I am sure you have some lessons under your belt already. Use them to buoy you up, rather than make you bitter. Rise above the negative thoughts and know that only you can define who you are and what you deserve in this life.

"Instead of putting others in their place, put yourself in their place."

– Amish Proverb

Chapter Eight

"I hope you never fear those mountains in the distance, never settle for the path of least resistance. I hope you dance."

– Lee Ann Womack

Resilience Learned from Friends

These stories were inspired by people in my life I love and cherish as friends. They were not able to tell their own stories. Two of them have passed away and the other still gets traumatized when trying to write about her experience, but she felt that sharing it was important and it might help other people. She gave me permission to tell the story for her. I am thankful for having these people in my life for both the joy and happiness they brought to our friendships, but also for what I learned from their resilience stories. I am happy to be able to share their stories here and hope you will learn something, as I did, from these beautiful souls.

Starfish Girl

I met my sweet friend, Lauren, in college when we were connected through mutual friends and ended up becoming roommates. It was unusual how quickly we became friends when we met and how deeply we connected, but we were going through emotional times of constant change, so maybe that was it. Lauren became a special friend partly because she picked me and was very definite about becoming my friend. Despite being a bit reserved, I have usually been the one to reach out and initiate friendships. Although, either way, it's the connection that develops that is important; being chosen does feel good and I always treasured that Lauren decided to pick me. We became roommates when my roommates from Hawaii, who I was sharing a house with, decided to go home for the summer and needed to save the prize location house, just a block from campus for fall quarter. I volunteered to stay and Lauren decided to move in and help save the house as well. We added a few other roommates that turned out to be an assortment of unique characters who became quite close by helping one another through a summer of fast-moving drama and trauma. Lauren met her future husband that summer and although their story turned out happily, it was not without plot twists and drama. One of our other roommates was a very shy friend who was learning to put herself out there a bit more and take chances in life. Another roommate was still in her teens. She had just found out she was pregnant and her boyfriend wanted nothing to do with having a child. One roommate was more worldly than the rest of us, with a true, hippy, free-spirit vibe dealing with sexual identity issues and substance abuse. You might guess that this led to an interesting summer with lots of drama. When the summer ended and our friends from Hawaii came back, Lauren and I decided to get an apartment a little further away from campus, where we lived for another year and became closer friends. Lauren eventually left for her student teaching and then graduated and got married. We stayed friends and I was happy to attend her wedding and see her start a new life. She was pregnant with her second child at my wedding and we stayed in touch through moves for many years, but eventually, life got ahead of us and we lost contact.

We reconnected in 2009, through Facebook. Unfortunately, Lauren's husband had passed away of an unexpected heart attack, just two months earlier. She was devastated but doing her best to move forward. Again, we connected quickly and I was happy to help her through those difficult times. One thing I noticed about my sweet friend, as she dealt with the loss of her husband, was that she was much stronger and wiser than the girl I had known in college, who had been more inclined toward drama and desperation. She had grown a lot during the years we had been disconnected. I am sure that comes with raising five children, four of them boys. She had moved many times, had experienced failed business ventures with her husband, had financial difficulties, issues with the kids, and had had an accident when she was pregnant with her youngest daughter, where she fell off a horse, hitting her head, causing traumatic brain injury. The recovery from that had been long and difficult and it left her daughter with some disabilities that made her dependent. Lauren had a different way of dealing with life than when I had known her many years earlier. She was so much more resilient, and it was a beautiful and hopeful resilience that was very positive. She had a very optimistic outlook on life and was determined to move forward towards something good. She did not want to be alone and I am happy to say she remarried in 2013, four years after her husband's death. She married someone she had known in grade school, who shared two important things that she loved and found to be anchors in her life: music and the Mormon faith she had converted to when she married her first husband. These two things, I quickly saw, were fundamental elements of the strong resilient woman I now knew and admired. It was great to see my friend happy and thriving in her new marriage and life. However, in 2017, Lauren became sick and first needed a hysterectomy and then gall bladder surgery. During the gall bladder surgery, they discovered cancerous tumors on her pancreas and liver. They were advanced, fast-growing, and not in a good location for surgery, so the prognosis was not good. Lauren put up a good fight though, as she truly loved life and wanted to live a lot more of it. She hoped to go on a mission with her husband and daughter to help just one more person. This, and her love for Loren Eisley's *The Starfish Story*, a poem I love as well, is the reason I have called her *"StarFish Girl"*. She told me how much she liked this poem when I visited her and spent the day with her in Spokane about nine months before she passed. At that time, she was hopeful. Since her middle is Hope, she always felt it appropriate to be hopeful. They were planning to reduce the tumors enough to lessen the risks of surgery through chemo and radiation. If it worked, they would attempt surgery. Lauren went through chemo and radiation and it did work enough to do the surgery. Things looked good, but then the cancer started growing again and spreading. Lauren got through all of this with her faith, her family, and playing music at church, as long as she could get there. We talked on the phone and she accepted the course that life was taking, still focused on the joy she found in small things. She was hopeful

for those she left behind and wanted to know they would be okay and live with love and respect. This was her main wish for her children, her husband Ron and her family and friends. She passed away in October of 2018, leaving behind a legacy of love. I know her family and friends miss her greatly, as I do, and I hope they learned some joyful resilience from her story too.

The Starfish Story - Loren Eisley

One day a man was walking along the beach when he noticed a boy picking something up and gently throwing it into the ocean.

Approaching the boy, he asked, "What are you doing?"

The youth replied, "Throwing starfish back into the ocean. The surf is up and the tide is going out. If I don't throw them back, they'll die."

"Son," the man said, "Don't you realize there are miles and miles of beach and hundreds of starfish? You can't make a difference!"

After listening politely, the boy bent down, picked up another starfish, and threw it back into the surf.

Then, smiling at the man, he said, "I made a difference for that one."

Lauren Nelson was a wife, mother of five grown children, grandmother, former teacher, pianist, piano teacher, and an active member of her church. She loved music, nature, and animals. She was a beautiful friend who is much loved and greatly missed.

The Joy of Being Maria

Maria Salomoa Schmidt was a force to be reckoned with, sometimes referred to as a "tsunami of love." She was strong-willed and made her presence known. Maria achieved more than most in her fifty-three years: raising five children; being a loving wife; a career as a spiritual coach and healer, speaker, author; and her life-long dream of being a guest on the Oprah Show. She led retreats and workshops, motivated people with live discussions on Facebook, and guided clients with her coaching practice. I connected with

Maria on LinkedIn in 2017. She contacted me about being on my radio show to talk about her book, *Finally Full of Yourself: Unlocking Your Spiritual DNA*. I wasn't sure what to think at first but soon learned that Maria was direct, straightforward, and genuine in her desire to spread and awaken the love she felt was within us all. I easily became friends with Maria. I was thrilled to meet her in person and spend the day with her in Boston in 2018, when I went to speak at the Integrative Wellness Symposium at the Harvard Faculty Club, at Harvard University in Cambridge, MA. She was warm and engaging in person and it was wonderful to spend time just hanging out and getting an in-person tour of some of her favorite Boston neighborhoods. After spending time with Maria, I truly understood her book and why she had been compelled to write it. It expresses a mindset and way of living life that Maria embodied, lived, and was excited to share. Maria and I stayed in touch and she did a Soul Talk, my video blog, with me on limiting beliefs. It was during this Soul Talk in 2018, that she revealed a disheartening secret and battle that she was fighting; she told us she had breast cancer and this was her second go-around with it.

Maria did not have an easy life. She was born in Portugal and experienced poverty and abuse early in life. She came to the United States as an immigrant child and was discriminated against and bullied growing up. She went through divorce, job loss, and discrimination in multiple forms. In 2008, she lost her infant daughter and was devastated by that grief. Maria rose above all of this with a determined and fighting spirit that held on to hope and love. She was determined to make something beautiful out of her hardships and pain, and she did just that. She became the joyful, loving human being that was called a "tsunami of love." Even so, adversity was not to be forgotten for Maria. After losing her daughter, she battled with breast cancer, going through the traditional therapies of chemotherapy and radiation, and thought she had won the the battle, only to have her cancer return in 2019. She was devastated, but hopeful. She had gone through a transformation in her beliefs and could not submit to the traditional Western methods for cancer treatment this second time around.

Her beliefs in energy and holistic healing were so strong that she had to follow her heart and be true to them. Maria was determined to keep living to the fullest as long as she was alive and leave a legacy of loving memories with those she left behind. It was her greatest wish that her family have experiences to remember and truly feel how much she loved them. She felt that traditional methods would take that away from her and rob her of the time she so cherished spending with her loved ones. Maria believed in laughter, hugs, dancing, creating, and sharing. She believed in joy in all its forms above all else. In our last interview on my radio show, *Soul Fire Wisdom*, she told me about the experience of building a custom chicken coop with her children. It was Maria's strong belief that these experiences done in love and laughter would be her legacy and that love would carry her loved ones through after she was gone. This was her resilience, living for almost a year longer than they predicted she would, she lived every moment fully. In July, 2020, I had Maria on my radio show/ podcast *Soul Fire Wisdom* for a longer show than normal;

it was called *The Joy of Being Maria*. Maria shared her wisdom and poured out her soul. She was still fighting and holding on to life then with all her might, however, I think we both knew what was coming. It is hard to let go and say goodbye to someone so beautiful and loving. Here is a link to the YouTube video for that show: https://youtu.be/SDB3o2UPBoM

Maria passed in January of 2021, leaving a wake of broken hearts, but also people who will never forget her heart-felt love and joyous spirit. Thank you, Maria, for the joy of your presence, your resilience, and your love!

Maria Salomoa Schmidt was a wife, mother of five children, realtor, author, speaker, holistic coach, and energy healer. Maria had a strong desire to make an impact and leave a legacy of love. There is no doubting that she did. She was a kind, loving friend who is greatly missed.

Mariko – Tsuyoi On'na

I met my friend, Mary, in college. She was a friend of and had gone to high school in Hawaii with one of my Japanese-American housemates. We became acquainted then and would talk at various gatherings, but never got to know each other really well. It would be decades later, in 2011, when we both moved to the same area around the same time, that our old college friend reconnected us. We started having lunches and got to know each other much better than we had in college. We became close friends and I knew her as a sweet, kind, thoughtful, shy but usually happy, confident woman. When I heard the news that she had been admitted to the hospital psychiatric ward for observation, I was extremely surprised. I knew that Mary sometimes had social anxiety and that she often worried about things, but I hadn't seen it as anything out of the ordinary. Talking with her husband, I found out that she had gotten to the point where she was pacing constantly, not sleeping, not eating, and they were very concerned for her welfare. I also found out that this had happened to some degree in the past and she had been diagnosed with bipolar disorder and PTSD. I knew something about her past, but she had not confided all of the details to me.

Leading up to the breakdown, Mary had gone through a rough time dealing with her and her husband's money issues as a result of job loss, and the death of her two beloved chihuahua dogs in close succession. The dogs were family members for a long time; she had nursed them through illness and disability, and she was devastated by losing them. The depth of her depression and anxiety had been worsened by her PTSD triggers, as well as losing her mother a while earlier, in addition to recovering from uterine and breast cancer that had impacts that were not fully healed.

Mary was born in Japan to an American Navy father and a Japanese mother. She grew up in Japan for the first twelve years of her life. She was torn and strongly influenced by and between the two cultures. She was abused as a child by her father and was perhaps confused by the culture and attitudes of her mother, whom she loved deeply. Her family eventually moved back to the United States, first to Hawaii and then to Bremerton, WA. She had many happy memories and connections to her childhood in Japan and had a strong connection both to Japanese ways and her Japanese family, with which she identified strongly. Adapting to her life in the US and fitting in as a Japanese-American, she tried to be what she thought was expected of her; there was a lot that Mary did not talk about. When I met Mary at Western Washington University, she was studying to be a teacher, like the majority of other students there. She left before graduating and married a young man she met while working at a hotel. He had originally come to the US from the UK and Scotland. They moved around a lot for her husband's job as an accountant and they had one child: a son. Mary did well in many ways helping to support her husband through college, eventually graduating from college in Florida herself, and working in the human resources field.

I was worried when I heard her stay in the psychiatric ward was extended beyond six weeks and she was not getting better. Eventually, she was moved to Western State Hospital in Tacoma. They were trying to get her out of the anxiety loop she was stuck in and get her medications balanced so she could start to function more normally, but things were going very slowly and nothing was working as expected. I found out later that Mary was aware of what was going on, on some level, but felt like she was observing it from outside of herself and didn't know how to reconnect. She was exhausted, but couldn't rest, she couldn't eat much and couldn't feed herself, she was paranoid and afraid of almost everything. She couldn't shower or dress herself and most normal functions were beyond her. Mary spent six months in Western State Hospital, which she remembers as a terrifying and strange experience with people she couldn't relate to. She felt trapped in a mind and in emotions that were not functioning for her. The process of getting back to functioning was slow and difficult, and she only remembers parts of it. Even after she was released from the hospital, there was a long road of processing, re-learning, and adapting to get back to functioning in her life. One very hard thing for Mary, and anyone who has had a similar experience, is dealing with why this has happened to you and being afraid that it will happen again.

It is a constant struggle to make sure that you are holding on to reality and functioning as expected. I know this to be true because my own mother had a mental breakdown caused by an interaction between two medications and was hospitalized for two weeks. She was always afraid it would happen again. Mary continues to struggle to live a healthy life and maintain her mental stability, as do many others who suffer with mental illnesses. She has learned many coping skills and practices to help her with this and make her more resilient. As well as keeping her medication in balance, she has learned to do things she enjoys, to keep connected to friends and her church, and to have creative pursuits. She loves music, singing, walking, cooking, gardening, and coloring to calm herself. She has learned the value of self-care and eating well. I am so proud of this resilient lady and how she has learned to deal with these adversities and thriveThis is why I have used her Japanese name in the title and call her "Tsuyoi On'na," which means strong woman in Japanese. When you think of those with mental illness, remember they are stronger than most of us. They are fighting a battle daily that we cannot even imagine.

Mary Bain is a wife, mother of a grown son, and currently retired from a career in human resources. She recently moved with her husband from Washington state to New Mexico, where she plans to continue healing, living life to the fullest, and pursuing the things she loves to live a joyful life. She is a beloved friend and I am happy to know her.

Chapter Nine

"No one escapes pain, fear, and suffering. Yet from pain can come wisdom, from fear can come courage, from suffering can come strength – if we have the virtue of resilience."

– Eric Greitens

Resilience Stories from Contributors

The stories in chapters nine through eleven are told by contributors I reached out to and asked to tell their stories. These are people who I saw something in the way they responded to difficult times, or in the stories they told about their experiences, that showed joyful resilience and some of the resilience traits I talk about in this book. I did not tell them what to write and some of them wrote about experiences or stories other than what I had seen or expected. They all have amazing stories of overcoming and getting through adversities. I hope that you will see in their stories the traits of resilience and the part that joy has played in the process for each of them.

The Resilience of Immigrants

In 2019, I invited a friend and colleague who I got to know through some speaking workshops to do a *Soul Talk* with me, a video blog I do that I mentioned earlier on in this book, and is just a conversation on a pre-selected topic. My friend was raised in the Ukraine, born in Germany, and her parents were interpreters. She became an interpreter herself and works with immigrants helping them to adapt. Dr. Larissa Chuprina got her doctoral degree in education, specializing in cross-cultural studies. We decided to talk about resilience and happiness, or joy because this was a topic we were both interested in for different reasons. Out of that talk, I realized that the experience of resilience, and specifically joyful resilience, was an area where a lot could be learned by looking at the immigrant experience. This is why I have included resilience stories from immigrants, including Dr. Chuprina, in this book. I hope the reader will see some of the beautiful resilience and joy I have seen in their stories.

I Could Only Talk to Dogs
by Dr. Anna Margolina

In 2008, my life seemed to be everything I ever desired. I, a person who grew up in the Soviet Union, now had a lovely house in America. Moreover, I had a husband, a cute white fluffy dog, two teenage daughters, and a baby boy. What else could I wish for! Yet, my soul was shrouded in darkness and I felt hopeless, exhausted, and defeated.

The problem was that in this new land, the United States, I now called home, nobody could understand me or was willing to listen long enough to form a human connection. One reason was my thick Russian accent. Another reason was a speech impediment called stuttering, which was so severe I couldn't even say my own name. What puzzled me, however, was that I never stuttered when I talked to dogs. If you have ever talked to a dog, you know they are wonderful people. They never judge. And they love you unconditionally with all your flaws and imperfections. I couldn't love myself. I didn't even like myself. I felt like a monumental failure.

Eventually, even my speech therapist ran out of options. I was seeing her every week in the hope of eradicating my stuttering. Every week, she produced a new tool meant to help me to speak with more ease, and every week, I failed to improve. I guess it was out of desperation that she decided to try something so out of the ordinary that, at first, I couldn't believe my ears.

"Anna, I want you to start stuttering on purpose."

"What?" My immediate reaction was to walk out of her office and slam the door. And yet, something inside of me wanted to grasp this last chance. After all, what did I have to lose?

So, one day, I decided to stop fighting my speech difficulties, but instead embrace them, accept them and even stutter on purpose. And there was a strange feeling; I had never experienced it before. It was a feeling of being in control. What was even more astonishing, my speech started flowing with ease. It was only for a brief moment, then stuttering resumed, but it was enough.

Suddenly, I could see it so clearly. I never stuttered when talking to dogs. It was easier to speak when I stuttered on purpose instead of trying to not stutter. I knew I had to find a way to learn how to teach myself to feel just as comfortable and confident around humans as I felt while talking to dogs.

First, I joined Toastmasters. Imagine how it felt walking toward the front of the room, getting ready to address an audience, knowing that I will stutter and it will be painful and embarrassing. My first speech, I couldn't even look people in the eye. I thought they would kick me out of the club. But they gave me a standing ovation.

After my first speech, I had to make myself do it again. And again. And again. And every time my heart was jumping to my throat, my knees were turning into jelly, with my chest feeling so tight I couldn't breathe. Finally, I had enough. "I will find a coach, a mentor, a magician – whoever can help me." So I found a neuro-linguistic programming specialist who helped me to reduce my anxiety. To my absolute delight, my speech also started flowing more smoothly. It was like magic. Aha! I was on the right path.

Over the next ten years, I became certified in neuro-linguistic programming, hypnotherapy, and a number of other healing modalities. And I became my first client, unraveling layers of trauma, healing wounds of my heart and soul. I also started taking improvisation, acting, and even clowning classes. I discovered that failures can become stepping stones to personal growth as long as I remembered not to let them stop me from moving forward.

Today, my speech is not completely free of stuttering. This old condition still visits me from time to time. Yet, today I can do things that seemed beyond my wildest dreams just ten years ago. I teach classes and seminars, speak at professional conferences, and coach private clients. Today, I know that my stuttering struggles do not define me and they certainly cannot stop me from performing big on life's stage. I no longer have to drag myself to speak kicking and screaming. I speak with joy, confidence and most importantly, I have fun.

Looking back, I can see a path full of painful failures. I shudder thinking how easy it was to just give up. And I feel grateful for my stubborn determination, which kept stepping, reaching, and at times crawling forward after each failure. Today, I feel grateful for stuttering. It became my gift, my motivation, and my wake-up call. Because of it, I know today with adamant certainty: I have a voice.

Dr. Anna Margolina, Ph.D. is a speaker, trainer, author, certified Tao instructor, master NLP practitioner, and hypnotherapist. She is the founder of Outdoor Hypnotherapy and Ageless with Anna. She combines science with a little magic and "woo" to achieve the best outcomes for her clients.

Survivor to Thriver
by Dr. Yvonne Kaye

It was September 5, 1939, and my family, all of them, were on holiday on a farm in Blean, just outside Canterbury, United Kingdom. Just short of my sixth birthday, war was declared. It was called World War Two as World War One was the war to end all wars. It didn't achieve its purpose and an entire generation was obliterated.

My family upped and left, saying it would be better to stay where I was. That was it. No explanation and I was the only one left behind. I didn't agree. I had to stay for six months. Going back to London at the beginning of 1940, the serious bombing began. We were bombed out twice and shattered again. I was sent away, then back, then sent away again until at eight years old I decided – enough! It's been that way ever since. That decision at eight years old has sustained me ever since.

London was in ruins. We all had to wear heavy full-faced rubber masks when there was an air raid. We had a little dog and he would run under the table about twenty minutes before the planes came with the bombs. It was relentless. We went into the cellar rather than an air raid shelter and waited until we heard the all-clear siren. It's somewhat like the siren that goes off when there is a fire in this country and I freeze when I hear it. Also, Beethoven's fifth symphony, that starts with *Da-Da-Da-Daaaa*. That was translated as SOS, so when we heard it, we were saved another day. Whenever I hear that music, I remember the relief.

My city was in a state of confusion. What to do? Where to go? Where was safe. We were rushed to a protected classroom when we were in school. I saw people killed in the streets, running from the bombing.

I was afraid. When I was eight and bombed out the second time, we were homeless and hungry. Rationing was punitive and on this particular day at eight years old something saved my life. People. They had little more than us, yet they took us into their homes, fed us with the little they had, and right in that moment I said to myself, "I want to be like that when I grow up!"

I am! What those people taught me was compassion, generosity, and most of all listening. We used to go into the houses that weren't bombed, and if there was a piano we would gather around and sing together, sometimes about Hitler and his thugs. There was a singer called Vera Lynn who was the heartbeat of the war, performing for the military. She was an influence on how to be, reminding us what was important. England's sweetheart. Her songs were filled with hope and love. One of her songs "The White Cliffs of Dover" was one of my favorites.

There'll be bluebirds over

The white cliffs of Dover

Tomorrow, just you wait and see

There'll be love and laughter

And peace ever after

Tomorrow, when the world is free

The shepherd will tend his sheep

The valley will bloom again

And Jimmy will go to sleep

In his own little room again

This song touched my soul. When I was taken away from London for a while, I imagined myself in my own little room again. It still does touch me when I think of it.

I took those horrific days and turned them into lessons. People ask me why I chose my profession, it was because of that war and the incredible earth angels that altered my life. Their courage astounded me, that there were people there who understood my fear and because of how many times I escaped death. How many people inspired me? Fourteen members of my family were in combat. My beloved John lied about his age, joined the Royal Navy, and went straight into combat at seventeen. That was many years before I knew him. Like many others, he never spoke of it, except to say that it was great fun! I can't recall any of the fourteen who volunteered to speak about their experiences either. Those who were not in that kind of combat were other relatives who became firefighters or air raid wardens who would check on whether the blackout curtains were up without any hint of light that would identify a house, building, or anything that could give the German planes any idea of a place to bomb. After a while, it didn't matter as they just bombed wherever they were. I learned lessons from all these experiences, which now allow me to work with people in enormous emotional pain, with PTSD, or with night terrors. I am so very honored to do so.

I dislike war intensely and will support the courageous men and women who protect us in wars created by people who never have to fight and stay at home safely.

My high school had a motto: *Amor Vincit Omnia*. It means "love conquers all." Mine is "be well and conquer!"

Dr. Yvonne Kay is a thanatologist living in Pennsylvania. She is a former radio host, who currently has her own podcast, a speaker and author. She has over fifty years of experience and specializes in bereavement and addiction counseling. She still loves working and helping people at eighty-seven years young. She likes to call herself a "queenager."

"You Are a Keeper!"
by Dr. Larissa Chuprina

In 2017, after five years of seemingly happy marriage, my world was shattered by a note from my beloved husband that he left on the counter for me on Easter Day when I was out for a church service in the morning. It said: "I have left you. I will send divorce papers later. You can keep the house and sell it to pay the debts."

That was like lightning in a clear sky. The day before, we had a nice walk on the beach and a romantic dinner together. And a week before that, we celebrated our fifth wedding anniversary, where I got a huge bouquet of flowers with a card saying, "You are a keeper."

During our marriage, my ex-husband would bring me flowers every second weekend with words, "I love you. I have been looking for you all my life." Once, he confessed that giving flowers to a spouse is a gesture for when children from a previous marriage are present as they need to adjust with time and attention. This way, the flowers show appreciation both for their children's acceptance and for their spouse's presence. Yes, I received flowers every other week when my ex-husband's son was staying with us. I loved the little guy and treated him as my own, which included giving him some critical eye or comments too, when I felt it was necessary. I was there for them both when his son was turning into a brilliant teenager, daring to take flight lessons, climb mountains, and play saxophone in the band.

My belief in the goodness of people and in the integrity of words and actions, when sacred words of LOVE are professed, was a foundation for my SELF-concept, which is, "I am loved, I am valuable, I am a loving human being."

My academic background in linguistics and career as a language specialist supported my belief that words have power. I was an avid follower of new age teachings with positive affirmations and meditation on love and kindness. I have a house full of books and notebooks filled with words of wisdom from numerous self-development classes. My favorite piece of research by Masaru Emoto is about water and its ability to respond to words. (*Messages from Water*, 1999). His research proved what I had known all my life, that positive, compassionate words have the power to comfort and heal, while negative words can hurt and even kill (the spirit). Thanks to the experimental work of Dr. Masaru Emoto, we see the frozen crystals of water, which confirms the healing power of positive thinking, uplifting speech, and prayer.

My revelation, about the power of the words and language we use when we speak to ourselves and others, just dawned on me after I prayed. I prayed for support and direction as to where to live, what to do for a living, and how to reinvent myself for a new role and the situation: I was divorced from my first husband, the father of my two children, and had just returned from the US where I had lived for eight years, to my home in Ukraine. My mother was still alive, and she took good care of our apartment. I could have gotten hired as a professor or translator with my good command of English, and I could have been happily settled down in my native country, where I had many friends and good professional connections.

What brought me to the United States was my curiosity and desire to expand my knowledge and opportunities. I was selected out of 800 candidates in Ukraine to be a Fulbright Fellow, thanks to my career in linguistics, teaching English as a foreign language, my interest in research, and experience running my language school for educational tourism. I found out about the program four days before the deadline, six months before I turned forty years of age, the cut-off age for applicants for the program.

I have always said, "If there is one percent of a chance to get something, I will give it a try!" This attitude, as I see it now, has helped me reach many seemingly unrealistic goals. My other saying to myself that helped me to get going and dream big was, "Put me anywhere, even on the Moon, and I will make it and create a beautiful life there." I sincerely believed it, and it worked like magic.

So, sitting in my old home, my apartment in Ukraine, surrounded by hundreds of dictionaries and books on linguistics and collections of world literature, I picked up one book and read a message for myself, "First was the Word.... Whatever you asked for... will be given!" And this was from my textbook on Old English! So, I asked in my prayer to be back in Tennessee, where my sons and my cat were at that time, to get a rewarding career, and feel limitless in my abilities by using the power of the words. Miraculously, I got all the necessary papers to get a US visa and a month later, was back at the University of Tennessee. Four months later, I got married and moved to the Seattle area, and got a visiting professorship position at one of the best universities there.

There are dozens of happy-ending stories in my life where a challenging situation ended up even better than I prayed for: help appeared, people showed up, money arrived, and opportunity presented itself. Though my life was not easy, it has always been interesting, full of adventure, and memories of people who played the role of an angel or a role of a teacher.

When I found the note that day, "I have left you..." for a moment, I lost myself and let a loud cry like a wounded bird, and then fell with wounded wings folding up. When I came back to myself, I felt like I either had a stroke or had been hit in my solar plexus very hard; I could not breathe for some time. It felt as if these words were imprinted in my heart. I felt numb and lifeless and lost trust in myself and my powers.

For months, besides the physical implications of getting high blood pressure and anxiety attacks, there was a worse consequence of these words: my mind tricked me as if it was separated from the divine. It affected my career, financial situation, and the relationship with my sons and my friends. I could not get a job, my tutoring business could not sustain me, I nearly lost my house, and I was in $50,000 debt after my divorce.

As soon as I caught myself in these negative thoughts, spiraling me down a rabbit hole, and all the underlying messages I was sending to myself, I did everything to get on the path to joyful resilience. First, I regained hope and trust in myself with my worth and my words. I joined Brain Body Yoga Tai Chi, a wellness studio, where I learned the ways to connect my body and brain; I learned mediation from the Art of Healing from the Master of Raja Yoga, and breathing techniques from the masters at Art of Living, promoting happiness and wellness. I put my focus on my dream to start a happiness foundation and start a movement for personal and societal happiness in the world. I coach English for the success and happiness of immigrants to help them to find their strengths and talents to realize their dreams.

Their stories of struggle and triumph continue to inspire me to be who I am and do what I do to spread the word and joy. I asked my students to write their stories down, as a record of their heroic deeds and as a reminder of what they have accomplished and overcome in a new culture with a language different from their mother tongue.

Rereading the stories of resilience written by immigrants to this country, I realized that it may be an immigrant trend to be resilient, however, it is an art of living and healing that helps us to be joyfully resilient. The proverbial saying "If you want to be happy, be!" proves to be useful in understanding that it takes conscious decisions to choose to be happy in times of adversity.

My struggles taught me to look at difficulties as learning opportunities and to focus on the solution while looking for something positive in each situation. This "trend" is also translated into a brand "English for Well-Being or Happiness" where I teach how to use the language that empowers them, inspires them, and creates better opportunities for a career, relationships, and self-growth. I have a passion for learning and teaching; like taking and giving, it provides me with balance, a mission, and a connection to a superpower.

My message to myself, "I will never leave you...Be strong and courageous. Do not fear or be in dread of them, for it is the Lord your God who goes with you. He will not leave you or forsake you." Deuteronomy 31:6 ESV. https://www.openbible.info/topics/i_will_never_leave_you_nor_forsake).

Dr. Larissa Chuprina is a translator who works with immigrants, an educator, and a researcher. She is also a happiness & positivity coach. She loves facilitating retreats and helping people to live happier lives. She lives in Kirkland, WA, and enjoys travel and new adventures.

Chapter Ten

Resilience Stories from Contributors

"Failure will never overtake me if my determination to succeed is strong enough"

– Og Mandino

The Resilience of Men

Men and women are called upon to be resilient in life with no gender bias, however, I have observed that in some ways they do respond to difficult times and adversity in different ways. Of course, it is a very individual thing and all people do respond to challenges in their own way. However, I think that there is some cultural conditioning in our society that influences, to some extent, how men and women feel they should and do respond to adversity. I would like to look more into this and see how those differences influence resilience and overall well-being in dealing with stress and adversity. I wanted to divide the stories by gender to see how these differences might be recognized and perceived by the reader.

Heartfelt Resilience
by Gary B. Larson

Tubes. Hoses. Cords. Tubes connecting hoses attached to cords. Gary kept seeing them. Hanging on walls, from carts, from beds. From bodies. Donna's body. Her face, neck, chest, stomach, finger.

In the past four days, they appeared in a recurring dream. Nope, they were real. Smooth and soft like a toothpaste tube. Others hard and stiff like a garden hose. Some like that slinky, bendy thing he played with as a kid – except these tubes, in the hospital, were coated in rubber.

Anyway. Gary woke up in that hospital waiting room. In the middle of the day!

Donna also slept there but down the hallway. Recovering from an operation. For open-heart surgery. He loved her treatment by the nurses, the doctors, the specialists. All their voices were as soothing as a rising tide in springtime. So clear about what they planned to do, what they were doing, what they have done.

Their care reminded him of his mom aiding the neighbor's kids. His work, before retirement, differed so much from theirs. Nothing hands-on about it. Keyboards separated him from the people he tried to help through writing.

"But shit, Gary," he whispered to himself. "This ain't about you."

It's about that food! He chuckled. Yeah, right. That salty food. In a hospital! In that bright, sterile, noisy cafeteria where he ate while Donna was in surgery or asleep.

All the people eating there. Scared and worried wives, husbands, children, and friends. Nurses and doctors in white. Nourishing their bodies. Getting a moment away from their worries, fears, stresses.

At least Donna didn't have to deal with that hubbub. But the smell of food in her room, the mysterious stuff served after her operation; it gagged her before she got well enough to order what she wanted off the menu.

Throughout the past forty-plus years, Gary had learned what Donna likes and doesn't like to eat, where she likes to eat, and what she likes to do after a romantic dinner with him celebrating something, anything, everything. Eating nurtured their relationship – even while he sat with Donna as food flowed into and out of her veins and arteries through tubes and hoses!

Also, during those years, Gary learned about Donna's heart murmur. The reason she was in the hospital. She'd mention it, such as when recalling her physical education classes in school. Such as when taking medication before seeing the dentist.

Gary worried about her heart because his mom had heart issues. She had died of them at sixty-one. His mother had always warned him that her health issues ran in the family. And sure enough, when Gary and Donna's youngest son was twenty-four, he suffered heart failure. But he survived. So did Gary after his heart failed at sixty-three. When Donna turned sixty-five and went on Medicare, her doctor recommended an examination to check the state of her heart. The exam revealed an aortic aneurysm. They learned that her cardiologist needed to repair an aortic valve. And insert a new bicuspid valve. And do two heart bypasses.

The day before surgery, Donna posted on Facebook: "Relatives and friends. Tomorrow I will be having open-heart surgery. It will be a while before Gary and I will be sharing walks, hikes, and other excursions with you."

The next day, he posted: "All my positive energy, thoughts, and feelings are focused today on the love of my life, Donna."

Of course, the thing he couldn't say: "I'm scared."

After five and a half hours of surgery, Donna's doctor told Gary the team accomplished all they had planned to do, "It went well. It all looks good!"

Gary's optimism jumped to joy. The headline across the front page of his life read "Our two hearts still pound together!"

And his joyful story to Facebook friends led with gratitude: "Thank you for your good vibes and 'Likes.' I've told Donna about her popularity and read her all the positive comments. She has been talking quietly from time to time, even smiling at some of my dumb jokes."

Gary's joy continued as he cared for Donna during her recovery at home. To prevent strain on the bones mending in her chest, Gary loved holding Donna as she stood, sat, lay down, and bathed without using her arms. He savored their strolls for Donna's heart. He shared photos of their walks, hikes, and other excursions.

And a year later, he loved posting on Facebook: "She met with her doctor today. 'She's doing wonderfully,' says the doc. 'And beautifully,' says me!"

Gary B. Larson and his wife, Donna, are enjoying retirement in Port Townsend, WA, after raising two sons in the Seattle area. Gary worked as a writer, editor for a newspaper, non-profit agency, and local government prior to retiring.

Surviving Cancer
by Ron Harrell

Early in 2019, I was diagnosed with prostate cancer. It was my third cancer diagnosis in twelve years. The biopsy that confirmed the prostate cancer diagnosis resulted in a four-day hospitalization with sepsis, followed by a ten-day regimen of intravenous antibiotics.

Once the dust settled on all that post-biopsy excitement, I started talking with the doctors—urologists and oncologists—about how to approach the diagnosis. In the end, there were basically two choices: 1) a prostatectomy or 2) forty-three daily radiation treatments followed by quarterly hormone suppressant therapy that would last two years. Understanding that the second option would be the least invasive, that was the road I chose.

Before beginning treatment, I was counseled by my radiation oncologist that the regimen I was embarking on was physically extremely taxing and that he strongly recommended that I see a physiatrist to begin working on an exercise program. The next day, I received a call from a physiatrist's office to schedule an appointment. So, I went.

After an assessment and a couple more visits, I put together a low-budget (but effective) mini-gym set-up in my garage and started working out. Gradually. Very gradually. I certainly was not testing my limits.

Then one day, about six months into the routine, I received an invitation from an old friend to participate in Monday to Friday, Saturday, and Sunday fitness challenges using an app associated with my wrist-borne fitness tracker. I figured, what the hell? Why not?

The decision to join in proved to be a powerful motivator. Before too many weeks had gone by, I was doing two forty-five-minute sessions on my exercise bike/elliptical plus five miles on the treadmill and a little weightlifting on the side every day. Over the next four months, I lost sixteen pounds and was feeling great.

Then, one day just before Christmas, as I was getting off the exercise bike/elliptical, I noticed a pain in my left foot. I could not think of anything I had done to injure it, but when I took off my shoe and sock, it was clearly bruised, red and swollen. I was lucky enough to get in to see my podiatrist the next day. He ordered lab work that ruled out gout, and then told me that he believed I had Charcot (pronounced "sharko") foot, a side effect of my diabetic neuropathy. Oh, I forgot to mention that I am a type 2 diabetic.

For the next eight weeks, my foot was in an immobilizing boot, I had x-rays and foot exams every other week, and finally, MRIs on my foot and ankle. I also was directed not to put weight on the foot or to walk, and to keep the foot elevated during that period. Plus, NO EXERCISING.

By the time I received the podiatrist's blessing to resume exercising, I had recaptured eight of those sixteen lost pounds, and I was far from my previous exercising accomplishments. I am gradually, so far successfully, building back up to it, but my wife has forbidden me from using the treadmill, convinced that the constant pounding of my feet was what had precipitated the Charcot foot episode. After thirty years of marriage, I know enough to defer to her better judgment. Still, I am getting back on track, and expect to be returning to a negative trajectory on my weight situation, getting that BMI back below thirty.

Reading back over this, I can see a number of jumping-off points for other stories of resilience that has helped pull me through several health crises. And for that resilience, I am grateful. The older I get, the more I realize that I will need to continue to rely on that resilience.

Ron Harrell is a sixty-seven-year-old retired Vietnam veteran, union representative, and industrial electrician. He lives just north of Seattle with his wife, Barbara, and their dog.

He has Type 2 diabetes and is a three-time cancer survivor who appreciates every day he has in this world. Growing up he was the curious boy down the street and now I see him as one of those inspiring resilience superheroes.

Living on the Edge
by Rocky Kandola

I came home late after a night with friends to see my father awake on the couch with a drink in hand. I knew something was off... it couldn't be happening again... I put my dog, Lassie, in my room, locked the door, and placed a shelf in front of the door. I laid down to sleep and didn't feel safe, so I put a hammer under the bed. I won't let them take me again... I'm seventeen years old, in Mississippi – the last time I was taken, I was twelve.

I woke up suddenly with cuffs on my wrists and ankle, with not even one second of confusion. I was surprised at how calm and casual I took it. They had broken quietly into my room, bypassing my security and capturing my weapons before restraining then waking me. I was stuck, kidnapped. I yelled for my parents once only to see the whites of their eyes peering through the gap in the door, they got me. Realization set in; I was a prisoner, once again.

The next months of my life in this program were a combination of fear, anxiety, torture, mental, physical, and sexual abuse. At twelve years old I endured the same program and my body automatically adjusted into survival mode. I had to say and do whatever was needed in order to get out of this place. The level of abuse I faced once again by the same perpetrators when I was twelve was equal, if not more. However, I was bigger and taller and wasn't going to be taken advantage of so easily. Unfortunately, as these systems are made to operate, they have a way of breaking even the toughest souls and biggest bodies.

I quickly set into a routine of physical fitness, being counted like an animal, violence, harsh language, harsher punishments, and focusing on graduating high school. For school, we would simply read a textbook and then take the test in the back of the book to receive grades and level up through the books to eventual graduation. It wasn't until four years later in college that the news reports came out that this school had false accreditations and my diploma wasn't even real.

Being totally isolated from the outside world with no ability to send mail without it being thoroughly inspected, I found a huge relief one day in a group session (the only time we were allowed to speak) when a case manager walked in and said, "Hey Rocky, do you know Chelsea from MS?" I was so happy to hear from a friend and couldn't believe that these people were allowing me to hear from her! As quickly as my elation rose, it was crushed. The case manager said, "She died, now sit down and get back to group." My entire world froze. I heard ringing in my ears. I felt as if all the wind was sucked out of me and my vision blurred. I started crying and shaking. Charles, a group mate, grabbed my shoulders and tried to hold me and comfort me. This was against the rules and he was taken away. The next days, I started to fall into a spiral of depression. I didn't know what I would be able to do to overcome this devastating news sitting in a boot camp prison with no way to reach out to anyone. I was ready to die myself. Not only because of Chelsea, but because of the pure injustice and meanness of the world I was living in.

Eventually while being so upset, I picked up a notepad and pen and started to write in a journal. Slowly, I started to find solace in communicating my thoughts (good and bad) to myself via this paper and pen. I would draw objects, hearts, names, and more. I wasn't allowed to speak to anyone nor make any calls or discuss these things in any letters.

As an adult, years later, I would look back at these writings and finally understand the powerful shift and knowledge I had gained from this experience. The power and ability to overcome the most difficult of situations and obstacles was always within myself. There is nowhere to look but inwards, and being forced to only journal about these thoughts that were making me sick and suicidal, made me more aware and able to move past them by myself, by writing to myself, and searching within for answers.

I experienced physical violence, mental torture, sexual abuse, and more, at nine different facilities all over the world before I was fourteen years old. After leaving that last school at seventeen, I thought I was done with being sent anywhere or being told to do anything by anyone. I dove into drugs, violence, street life, women, partying, and everything that society didn't condone. I felt untouchable after finally escaping all the trauma of my teen years and was ready to make the world pay for my pain. That only brought me ten times more pain and horrible near-death situations, including adult prisons, institutions, and hospitals. It wouldn't be until nearly ten years later that I once again would decide to shift my state and look within myself. I once again picked up that paper and pen and began where I left off...

Rocky Singh Kandola is the owner of Hair Maiden India and is a speaker, author, and coach. He is also a convicted felon who has found his way back from a life of mistakes, adversity, and difficult circumstances. He lives in Los Angeles, CA, and continues to find his own path and share his story to help others find theirs.

My Resilience
by Frank King

Depression and suicide run in my family, it's called "generational depression and suicide." My grandmother died by suicide, my mother found her. My great aunt died by suicide, my mother and I found her. I was four years old, and I screamed for days.

And I've come close enough to dying by suicide that I can tell you what the barrel of my gun tastes like...literally. Spoiler alert: I did not pull the trigger.

I'll spare you the details of my great aunt's suicide, as they are (trigger warning), horror movie gruesome, however, if you'd like to know her story, and that of my grandmother, both are in my first (of six) TEDx Talks on mental health called "A Matter of Laugh or Death": https://youtu.be/aBUXND5BD4M

I live with two mental illnesses/superpowers (more on the superpower part in a minute). One is major depressive disorder, which is relatively common and generally not situational, however, a situation can trigger it, hence my close call with death at my own hand, again, literally.

The situation was the Great Recession, thank you George W. Bush, and the big banks. By 2010, my speaking business had dropped off by 80%, I had run through all my lines of credit, and I had driven my credit scores, not just into the ground, I had driven them into Middle-earth. To survive financially, we did what millions of Americans (and others) did, we filed for bankruptcy, losing everything we had worked to build in our twenty-five years of marriage, and I had (trigger warning) an itch on the roof of my mouth that I could only scratch with the front sight on my nickel-plated Ruger .38, loaded with Federal Hydra-Shock hollow points. My odds of surviving pulling the trigger were roughly the same as injecting Clorox to kill coronavirus. Slim, and who's his next of kin?

The bankruptcy devasted my wife, and she (logically) blamed me, as I had always "managed" the money. Honestly, if you lived through that time period, you are probably aware that Lehman Brothers, Goldman Sachs, and the good folks at Moody's who rated those toxic bundled mortgages, had a lot more to do with it than I did. For context, I recommend "The Big Short," though the finances discussed are so Byzantine that you may have to watch it more than once to understand it. Watch it at: https://www.imdb.com/title/tt1596363/.

What I understood was that my wife was suffering, and I had a solution - suicide - (which for me is always a solution, for problems large and small, but more on that in a minute as well) as I had a one million dollar life insurance policy.

As with many who are suicidal, I felt as if I was a burden to my wife, given that I was worth more dead than alive, literally. She would be broken-hearted, but she would not be broke. She would be restored financially.

The catch was, I knew that my life insurance policy had a two-year suicide clause. Meaning, if I killed myself any time in the first twenty-four months that I'd had the policy, the insurance company would pay nothing. After twenty-four months they'd pay in full.

I had had the policy for twenty-two months. I had to wait two months to die.

That was not a problem. You see, my second mental health condition, far more rare than major depressive disorder, is chronic suicidal ideation. Don't feel bad if you've never heard of it; a number of mental health clinicians that I've mentioned it to had no idea what it was. They'd stare at me, like Kim Kardashian, staring at the *New York Times* crossword puzzle.

Apparently, it's not in the DSM (I guess it doesn't exist...don't get me started), so to some, it doesn't exist. To those of us who have it, it's very real. What it means, for me and people in my tribe, is that the option of suicide is always on the menu, as a solution for problems, large and small.

And when I say small, a couple of years ago when my car broke down, I had three thoughts unbidden: I could get it fixed, buy a new one, or I could just kill myself. That's chronic suicidal ideation, in a nutshell, pardon the pun.

So, I was able, though unwilling (refused to leave my wife without resources), to kill myself at twenty-two months, but I could also wait until twenty-four months, when the life insurance policy would be fully in force, because of my superpower—suicide.

I say superpower because, since I pretty much live in the exit row on the airplane of life, in the window seat, and can pop the door open at any time to bail out of my earthly existence, I can end the pain any time I choose. Knowing this, it wasn't difficult to live those additional two months because at that point I knew that I could end the pain.

That's what a lot of people don't understand about suicide. I believe that it is most often the case, that the person does not want to kill themselves (I didn't), they just want to end the pain. And because I am willing and able to do that any time, any place, anywhere, I can stand a great deal of pain, knowing that I have the power to bring it to an end at any time of my choosing. Ironically, my chronic suicidal ideation helps keep me alive, thus, it's one of my superpowers.

I know what you're thinking, "Wait a minute, the title of this little diatribe is 'Resilience.' How does that tie into all of this?" Glad you asked.

Neuro-typical people often believe that the key to preventing someone from dying by suicide is to teach them resilience. There are speakers and trainers who make their living doing resilience training, to prevent suicide. And though their hearts are in the right place, their view of the role of resilience in suicidality is skewed at best, and dead (pun intended) wrong at its worst.

The most resilient people I know, are those who are most depressed and suicidal because if they weren't, they wouldn't still be here. As a matter of fact, rather than have the depressed and suicidal take classes in resilience, we should have them teaching classes in resilience.

Finally, I had to use my suicide superpower last fall to save our eleven rescue kitties from possibly dying in a wildfire. The fire was moving fast toward our neighborhood and was roughly a mile and a quarter from our house. I was in town about twenty-five minutes away when the alert on my phone told me that our neighborhood was being evacuated, immediately. It said we were at "level 3." If you've not been through a wildfire, level 1 is "get ready," level 2 is "get set," and level 3 is "get the f**k out, take nothing, just jump in your car and haul ass."

Well, we are like the Marines, we never leave a man (or woman, or kitty) behind. So as everyone else was leaving the neighborhood, I was driving in. A friend of mine said, "You could have died." That's true. What he didn't know was I could not have lived if they had died in that fire and I had not tried to rescue those cats. Besides, I'm suicidal, it's my superpower, so what did I have to lose? And if you have to die, what better way to go than in an attempted rescue of eleven defenseless kitty cats.

And my friend also said, "You could have died in the fire, burned up!" No, that wouldn't happen, that's no way to go. If the fire were licking my shoes and it appeared I was going to burn alive, I still have my nickel-plated .38, with those Federal Hydra-Shock hollow points. Before becoming a crispy critter, I'd have ridden one of those bullets over the "rainbow bridge" with my pack. How's that for resilience? The good news is, we all survived, as did the house. And I recorded a video on my iPhone as I made my way out of the neighborhood, wondering aloud if we'd make it. I had gotten all eleven into carriers, and into the car (I gained a whole new level of respect for the expression "herding cats," as I shoved one in a carrier, two would jump out).

Suicidal as I am, as I always am, I'm glad to be alive to share it, even though I cry as I watch it again... Here's the video "Cat Daddy to the Rescue": https://youtu.be/PgKQnbUV1GU.

Frank King is a suicide prevention speaker, a TEDx speaker coach, a stand-up comedian, and author. He was a writer for twenty years for the Tonight Show. He lives in Oregon with his wife and a large family of rescue animals including ten cats.

Mental Health

In light of the seriousness of the topic of mental health and the need to talk about it more, I want to say a few words here. Mental health is a concern and issue in our society today that is becoming increasingly deadly and needs our attention. It needs to be talked about more, normalized, and dealt with, as does our physical health. We need to protect and nurture our mental and emotional well-being as much as our physical well-being. While we aim to promote and strive for wellness in all areas, we also need to promote appropriate treatments and interventions for mental and emotional disorders and traumas when things have gotten out of balance. Below are some resources we need to be familiar with and use when needed.

National suicide Prevention Hotline: 1-800-273-8255

https://suicidepreventionlifeline.org/

SAMHSA National Helpline – Mental Referral Service – 1-800-662-4357

Chapter Eleven

Resilience Stories from Contributors

"She stood in the storm and when the wind did not blow her away, she adjusted her sails."

– Elizabeth Edwards

The Resilience of Women

This may be a bias on my part, but I have always thought that women are more naturally resilient than men or at least possess a quality of resilience that men less often seem to have. It is a subtle softness and ability to bend and be more malleable, generally speaking, than men feel the need to be. I think it is because men are generally seen to be stronger in a physical sense that women have sought to develop their strengths in other ways. This is just supposition and something to think about as you read the resilience stories of both men and women.

Steering Curiosity
by Marcelle Allen

Growing up I was given everything I needed. I had love, direction, and basketball shoes. You could say I was spoiled and supported by a loving family. My dreams were huge and my skills didn't match. My imagination and ability to see the big picture of possibility didn't always get along with logic and reality.

During college was an exciting time for me. I explored my faith, the beautiful parks in Bellingham, WA, and I tried my hand at a long-distance relationship. Upon graduation, I ventured out into the real world and got a big job. I hated it. Hard work wasn't the part I hated, I valued discipline and teamwork. It was a perfect storm. A new city, new apartment, new schedule, and a lot of dark phone calls with my boyfriend who was fighting a war in Iraq.

I didn't always know how to set boundaries. I was an excellent listener. I heard his war stories. I could picture the terrible things he shared with me. His nightmares became mine. I was doing my best to be "all corporate" and charming in the cold office environment, but I was developing an inner dialogue that I couldn't control. Our brains are so powerful and I didn't realize how dangerous my own thoughts would become. My imagination twisted his stories with my own disappointment at my job.

Eventually, I began asking depressing questions like, How can I escape? What if I wasn't here? The trick with your brain is that it will answer any question you ask it. Even though I had been seen as a positive and inspiring force in my community and I had a quote or scripture to motivate or inspire anyone, I didn't realize the damage my own curiosity was doing to my soul.

Let's just say I eventually got a two-week glimpse of the inside of a psych ward. I didn't really belong there, but I enjoyed doing puzzles for hours. I thought a lot about my life and how terrible the decor was. I had become so critical. I wasn't always critical; I just saw potential in people and places. Looking back now, I realize I was out of rapport with my own mind; I didn't blame him, the war, or the corporation. I was a creative who hadn't learned a few essential life skills yet. They told me I could get a psychiatrist or a life coach because I was no longer a threat to myself. I chose a life coach. I was an athlete in school and my coach was such an inspiration for me that it seemed like a perfect fit. He helped me trust my brain again and to befriend it with good questions. Learning that our brains are like search engines saved my life. I began to use good curiosity. Empowering questions like, What was good about my day? How can I serve? What pattern could I shift to improve my results? Who else do I need on my team? The majority of my YouTube videos are questions to steer others and myself in a positive direction. Dreamsity.com was created to tickle the imagination of other big dreamers.

People come and go in our lives, but our relationship with our own mind is ongoing. Our ability to navigate our imagination, honor our soul, and lead our actions is a skill in curiosity and mindfulness that we can all embrace. I call it productive pondering. I invite you all to ask well and stay well.

Marcelle Allen is a laughter coach, author, and numbers nerd, who supports creative professionals to understand *sales systems and marketing translating into big money. Her consulting agency book, <u>Financial Joy: Know the Data Behind Your Dreams</u>, makes her a go-to expert clients count on to smile all the way to the bank.*

How I Learned to Strengthen My Resiliency Muscles
by Edie Weinstein

I call myself a resilient thriver, who has not only survived challenges in my sixty-two years but expanded my life and created opportunities that would not likely have presented themselves without first walking through the fire that purified me, even as it metaphorically singed me a bit around the edges. The second quality of those who see themselves not as victims, but indeed thrivers, is that they use their experience to help others.

I come from resilient stock. My paternal grandparents were Russian Jewish immigrants who traveled to America before the pogrom. I saw the can-do attitude modeled by my parents, Selma and Moish. Both had lost their fathers relatively early in their lives. My mom was eighteen when my grandfather Edward, for whom I was named and my dad was thirty-two when his father, Jacob for whom my sister Jan was named, died. Until her death when I was four, there was not a time when my grandmother and mother were apart. I have no recollection of my mother's reaction to her passing, but I know she missed her daily and carried her spirit with her. I saw my grandmother in her and now see my mother in me. She was the rock on which everyone leaned, and I can imagine she learned well from her mother and, in turn, that role was passed on to me. Toward the end of my mother's life, I reminded her that rocks crumble. It was a hard-fought lesson that took me many years to absorb.

In 2018, I took the journey of a lifetime to Ireland and while there, had the chance to literally release that responsibility into a massive, smooth rock in the middle of standing stones. I called it the Mama Rock and as I embraced it, I felt an extraordinary sense of relief as if I had exhaled for the first time in ages. I then turned over and stretched out over it, with my face to the sun. Tears streamed down my face for all the times I wanted to receive love and support but was reluctant to ask since I was more at ease in the caregiver role. When I walked out of the circle, I felt a sense of rebirth.

As I gaze down at my left hand, I see a symbol of the indelible bond between them and, in turn, their granddaughter and daughter. It is a pinkie ring that had been downsized from my maternal grandmother's engagement ring. She gave it to my mother, and before she died in 2010, my mother gave it to me.

In some women's circles I have been part of, we recite our names and then our female lineage. I am Edie, daughter of Selma, granddaughter of Henrietta and Rebecca, great-granddaughter of Molly and Ada. These were strong, resilient women who raised their children well, with a solid work ethic and social conscience. Such were the seeds that blossomed into my own healing, and peace and social justice work. I sense that all of the ancestors are gazing down in appreciation for the evolution of Edie, knowing that a part of each of them lives on in me. In Yiddish, the word is *kvell*, which means to beam with pride. I know that they love their grandchildren (my sister has three children and two grandchildren, and I have one child and now a grandchild) who are part of their story too; more leaves on the family tree. My parents were alive until our children were grown, and they have fond memories.

It is to family and friends I have turned when life got "lifey." In 1992, we experienced what I lovingly call our "year from hell." In March, I had an ectopic pregnancy, a fallopian tube ruptured, and I nearly hemorrhaged to death. In May, my husband was diagnosed with hepatitis C and we began a journey that ended with his death in 1998. In August, we lost our house in Homestead, Florida, to Hurricane Andrew. We moved back to the Philadelphia area and Michael's illness progressed slowly. A doctor friend had advised us that this form of liver disease was like rust that eats away at the structure of a bridge. It may take time, but if not successfully treated, the bridge would collapse. That it did.

On November 11, 1998, Michael entered Thomas Jefferson University Hospital for the final time, after multiple trips since his diagnosis. He was comatose and immediately put on a ventilator. For five and a half weeks he was in the ICU and I lived there with him, not sleeping at home until the day he himself went home. Each night I did my best to pray him into wellness as I did what I called God-wrestling. "He's mine and you can't have him," I would declare, to which the divine would answer, "No, he's mine and he's on loan to you like everyone else in your life." That message remains with me to this day, as I treasure everyone in my circles. The morning that Michael took his final breath, I was with family and a few friends gathered around his bedside, as my decision to disconnect life support became a reality. It was a choiceless choice. He had been waiting for a liver transplant that never occurred and his body was too weary to continue without it. The rust had broken through.

At the moment the flatline appeared on the monitor, I heard what I refer to as "the voice" that said, "Call the seminary and ask to finish what Michael started." I knew exactly what that meant. He had been enrolled in The New Seminary with the goal of being ordained as an interfaith minister. I casually studied along with him, little knowing that I was being prepared too. I had no interest in taking on the mantle of clergy. But I read to him, typed his papers, quizzed him, watched the videos, and listened to the tapes. I even sat in on the conference calls. A few days after his Christmas Eve funeral service, I did indeed call the school. I was told by the loving and supportive dean, Diane Berke, that I could join them and graduate with Michael's class on two conditions. The first was that I was doing it for myself and not just for him and the second was that I had to do both the first and second year's work simultaneously or wait until the following year. I completed two years' worth of material and requirements for ordination in six months. In June of 1999, I walked down the aisle of the Cathedral of St. John the Divine in NYC and fairly floated my way out as a newly minted Rev.

My skills have been called upon countless times since then as I've officiated at nearly 400 weddings and numerous funerals, including those of my beloved parents. My father died in 2008 of Parkinson's disease and my mother followed him in 2010, her life ended by congestive heart failure, but I am certain, also of a broken heart. I think of them as eternal sweethearts who are still dancing in the kitchen which was one of the secrets to the longevity of their marriage. Tonight, I said Kaddish (the Jewish Mourner's Prayer) for my father since this is the thirteenth anniversary of his passing. I miss them dearly and feel their presence daily. Such is the paradox of death.

In 2018, I accompanied yet another loved one to the edge, as my friend Ondreah was nearing the end of her time in this realm, readying herself to transition to the next. She was diagnosed with triple-negative breast cancer and as a nurse had only surface knowledge of what that would mean for her remaining time. She used it well, as she found ways to cope with the uncertainty. She referred to her condition as "getting on the C train." Her chemo was called "IV meds," on the tubing, she would put Post-it notes with affirmations on them. She had her accouterment with her each time, which included music, her prayer beads, and photos of her spiritual teacher to place around the room at the hospital. She educated the staff who, amazingly, had never seen anyone like her. Seeing that reminded me of how I would decorate Michael's hospital room, so the staff would view him as a person and not a body in a bed. Her last breath was taken in an inpatient hospice. Holding vigil that night was her sister, brother, and a few other friends. Her elderly parents had come by earlier to say their farewells. At nearly 1 a.m. on December 9, I felt the essence of who she was slip away. Tears of sorrow, relief, and love flowed. I had touched the infinite. Although we were not lovers, she was the closest thing to a partner that I had in many years. As is so with my parents, and with Michael, and all of the others in my life who have crossed over into the beyond, it seems as if they too are part of my resilience, remaining with me in memory, and sometimes my dreams.

With each event and every detour from the road I thought I was supposed to be traveling, my emotional elasticity muscles became more flexible. Call me an Olympic-level resiliency gymnast. Ready for a gold medal.

Edie Weinstein is an author, speaker, journalist, and former radio host. She lives in Philadelphia, PA, and is a licensed social worker. She is the founder of Hug Mobsters and calls herself an Opti-Mystical and Bliss Mistress. She is a mom and grandmother to a beautiful grandson she adores.

A Time to Die
by Dara Lee

Six years ago, I decided to die. I'd struggled against suicide for years, trying to find something that would make it possible to go on living. I no longer even dreamed of being happy someday. For a while, I would have settled for a neutral existence while waiting for my life to run itself out, but I'd even given up on that.

I was exhausted by the sheer effort it took to stay alive, every moment struggling against suffocating fear. It required constant vigilance to maintain the strategies that calmed me. More than once I'd used those strategies to build a life that appeared almost normal from the outside. But eventually, I lose my iron grip on "normal" and my carefully constructed life burns to the ground again.

Eventually, a word was put to that horror: complex PTSD. Giving it a name never helped much. It was just a code word everyone pretended to understand, a way of saying what was wrong with me in two words instead of one hundred. I got treatment and drugs, then more treatment and different drugs. But what was happening *inside* me never ended. That's the nature of PTSD.

I was a good patient. Therapists praised my progress, my stellar ability to cope. My PTSD was at the top of the chart, similar to highly traumatized combat veterans, yet when things were "good" I could appear semi-normal. When I protested it wasn't a life worth living my therapist admonished me to be grateful - there was no cure for PTSD, most folks couldn't hope for the functionality I had.

My decision to die brought an overwhelming sense of relief I hadn't felt in years. The only thing that stood in my way was getting my disabled mother into assisted living. I sometimes feared I couldn't hang on long enough to make sure she was safe before leaving her alone. On those days I'd make the "tomorrow-bargain." Tomorrow I could kill myself, just not today.

Some days even the tomorrow-hard-wired-for-fear bargain didn't work and I'd have to distract myself with complex videos until the compulsion passed. On one particularly bad day, I found a university lecture about the hard-wiring of the brain in compulsive thought disorders. I concentrated on the professor as hard as I could.

He explained that when we keep thinking the same thoughts our brain begins producing those thoughts automatically. Live in fear long enough and the brain stops being able to produce anything but constant fear - forever. Our brain is now, incapable of being anything else. I suddenly understood: I was no longer in control of my brain; my brain had taken control of me.

The lecturer said it was impossible to make the brain stop thinking a hard-wired thought. Even drugs couldn't stop it, only suppress it a bit. Then he said the words that changed my life: "We can't make it stop, but we *can* teach it to do something different."

I was stunned. My beliefs were wrong. I didn't have to be grateful I could sometimes function through misery; I could be cured. I had no idea how to do it, absolutely none, but I knew it was possible. The first thing I did was write my own permission slip, permission to get well. No one could show me the way, I had to find my own way. I'd been a model patient, gotten an "A" for effort across the board. But when experts declared there was nothing more to do, I'd done nothing more. They said there was no hope for anything better, so I'd given up hope. There was no gatekeeper who held the key to my recovery. I had to become my own key.

I decided right then and there I would give myself a year to live, a year dedicated to finding my own answers. The thought first thrilled me, then fear flooded back. How could I stand another year? I reminded myself of the tomorrow-bargain. I could change my mind tomorrow. But just for today, I was going to give myself a year to find my own key to the gate of freedom.

I quit work to study brain plasticity full-time, diligently implementing everything theory. I discovered I couldn't retrain my brain part of the time, I had to be absolutely vigilant with my thoughts, conversations, and outside input every minute. I continuously turned my thoughts away from my hard-wired fear and despair, toward opposite thoughts. I tried every suggestion, continued what helped, and discarded what didn't. Through trial and error, I rewired my own brain.

In a nutshell, I turned my focus away from my "problem" and toward where I wanted to be. I eliminated all outside negativity, listening only to comedy and inspirational media. I cut out everything with advertising because commercials are all based on fear and lack. I had to listen to the good stuff continually or my brain would head right back to its hard-wired thoughts of doom.

I developed a daily gratitude and meditation practice. I found affirmations that worked and said them several times a day. I started journaling about how my life was going to look as it transformed, practicing the new way I'd feel. I walked every day. I noticed and named everything that was good. I found photographing the good I was discovering helped me to stay focused. I bought Easy Buttons from Staples and put them everywhere, hitting them each time something went well. I discovered most traffic lights were green, it had only seemed like they were all red because that was all I'd ever paid attention to.

Being diligent and focused every waking moment was exhausting. I feared it might be an impossible task. Was I fooling myself by believing I could do what everyone said couldn't be done? My brain wouldn't stop with the constant crap. Who was I to think I could do this?

I remember vividly the very first time my brain had a non-PTSD thought on its own, without me having to consciously and purposefully form it. I glanced down the hall, noticing the flowers outside the window. My brain said, without any conscious prompting from me, *That's beautiful.*

I stopped in my tracks. I couldn't remember the last time my brain had a thought about anything other than past tragedy, what was wrong in the now, disasters looming in the future, or how to prevent them from happening. It had taken only a few weeks to see my first results. Exhausting and frustrating weeks, but relatively nothing after decades of PTSD-induced despair.

Within a year my life was completely transformed. As I continue to evolve my practices, every year gets even better. I'm a passionate hiker, road-tripper, photographer, and writer. I've become a reiki master and teach meditation. I'm surrounded by people who love me. I'm regularly called an inspiration. I'm deeply content and joyous from the inside out.

Miracles only happen when we step beyond the confines of what everyone else believes. Stop waiting for someone to hand you the key. Become your own gatekeeper. Find your own way.

Dara Lee is a reiki energy healer and coach dedicated to radical self-empowerment. She is a lover of nature, a writer, and photographer. She lives in Washington where she spends much of her time exploring the outdoors.

Part Three

The "How?"

Chapters twelve through fifteen show you how and give the tools and techniques to embark on your own journey turning resilience into joyful resilience and to live a healthier, happier, and more fulfilling life. The practices, tools, and resources in these chapters are meant to be used in conjunction with the journal "Simple Soul Thoughts: Collecting Moments of Joy." The bonus gifts will give you some extra enhancements and tools for your own transformation journey.

Chapter Twelve

"Although the World is full of suffering, it is also full of overcoming it"

— Helen Keller

Creating Mindset

One of the most important factors in being resilient and joyfully resilient is creating or shifting our mindset. First, we need to define exactly what we mean when we refer to mindset.

It is generally accepted that mindset is the set of beliefs that form how we make sense of and see the world around us and how we function or fit into it. It influences how we think, feel, and act in every situation.

It is important because it affects our self-talk, thoughts, all of our beliefs, actions, attitudes about ourselves and how we should behave in relation to others and our environment. It is our construct or operating system for navigating the world and everything and everyone we encounter in it.

I like to look at the neuroscience explanation as it is becoming one of my favorite areas of study for understanding the "why" of human behaviors. Mindset originates in the cerebrum of the brain, which contains the right and left hemispheres of the brain. Neurons carry signals or messages and form neural pathways that go out to both sides of our brain to form the thoughts and eventually actions and behaviors we engage in. Repeated thoughts form those neural pathways which over time become patterns of choice or behaviors we return to when we encounter the same stimuli. To break it down, if we think that something is true or re-enforce our belief in a thought repeatedly, automatically when anything associated with that is encountered, we build our reactions and subsequence associations on that belief. If we believe the Earth is round, all of our subsequent logical associations, reasoning, and assumptions will be based on this underlying belief. Mindset is made up of a set of these types of underlying and repeatedly accepted truths or beliefs.

How is Mindset Created?

Mindset comes from our experiences, our education, our culture, and to some extent from the information we take in from sources such as media and books. It is something that grows and changes with added information and new experiences, in most cases, if we are open to allowing new information and experiences. It forms a framework for our attitudes and actions that can be shifted or reframed. Usually, mindset is something that comes about naturally, by what we encounter and are exposed to in our lives, however, knowing how important it is and what a significant effect this has on our lives, mindset can also be purposefully shifted in a number of ways to help us be in our most resourceful state. Some ways that can help you create or shift mindset are:

1. Find an example or model of the mindset you would like to achieve
2. Imagine yourself with the thoughts and feelings you'd like to have
3. Believe that you think in those desired patterns
4. Experience the outcomes that you would expect
5. Make time and space for what you desire
6. Act in alignment with this thinking
7. Practice gratitude
8. Breathe into and feel it with all of your senses

There are also some tools that can help in this process. These are intentions, affirmations, and mantras, as well as normal functions such as thoughts, self-talk, and actions, or behaviors.

Setting an intention means stating what you intend to accomplish by certain actions or a set of actions or steps. You are making a commitment to move in a certain direction to get to a specific outcome. It helps narrow the pathway and steps needed, and therefore aids in forming or shifting mindset. Some examples of setting intentions that might help in forming mindset would be:

1. I intend to see the good in people.
2. I intend to speak only positively.
3. I intend to see the best possible outcome.

These might be intentions that would help in forming an optimistic or positive mindset. It is not just a matter of saying the intention but stating it and then making the effort to take action on it. It is a process that takes action and practice.

Affirmations are another powerful tool in creating mindset. An affirmation is a positive statement that can aid in overcoming negative self-talk and self-sabotaging thoughts or attitudes. First, we need to realize and be aware of the negative self-talk and thoughts we are feeding ourselves, then decide what we'd like to change. You make an affirmation that you can repeat regularly that challenges and negates the self-talk or thoughts you want to change. There are a few rules that help make your affirmations effective:

1. Start with the power phrase "I am." This makes it both personal and powerful.
2. Always use the present tense.
3. Make it short and sweet.
4. Feeling statements help to get to the core of things.
5. Be realistic
6. Expect change.

Affirmations can be effective in reprogramming the subconscious mind. After all, we have been programming our mind with our negative and self-sabotaging statements, we need to replace those with the more positive desired statements. Some examples of affirmations are:

1. I am smart.
2. I am kind.
3. I am deserving.

Used properly, affirmations can be very empowering and help us to reduce stress and anxiety. Repeated over and over, they take control of your thought patterns, slowly changing your thinking to more desired patterns, and rewire the neural circuits so that these new thoughts and self-talk are your automatic go-to.

Mantras can also be helpful. A mantra is a sound, slogan, or statement repeated frequently to maintain focus. It is commonly and often used in mediation. Many people think affirmations and mantras are the same, but they are not. Affirmations are positive statements to help you reprogram your mind or mindset. Mantras are sounds or statements meant to focus and motivate you. They can both be helpful in forming, shifting, and maintaining mindset, but they are used differently and have different functional results. A few examples of mantras are:

1. All I do is win!
2. I can and I will!
3. Everything happens as it should!
4. I believe in me!
5. Ohmm!

Repeated daily, these mantras can help to motivate and focus you and thus create the mindset you are working toward. To build a resilience mindset you are building the traits listed in earlier chapters that help us to deal with and bounce back when faced with adversity and difficult times. To build a joyful resilience mindset you are building those traits along with a core or reservoir of joyfulness by collecting, seeking out, and constantly returning to moments of joy in your life. Therefore, setting an intention to be joyful and see joy and blessings in your daily life, having some affirmations around joy or joyfulness with a mantra that keeps you focused on joy and joy seeking would all help you in creating your joyful resilience mindset. It is a process and a practice, not something that is one and done. Don't expect immediate results, but if you work on it, you can make big changes and get powerful, lasting results fairly soon,.

Mindset has been categorized into two primary types: a fixed mindset and a growth mindset. With a fixed mindset, people do not believe they can change, so they tend not to try. They resist change and basically block new information. Those with a growth mindset believe they can change and grow, therefore they are more open to change, risk and challenges. With these two basic categories, there are many subsets of mindset; the study of mindset and how it works is quite extensive. For the purpose of looking at mindset's impact on resilience and joyful resilience, it is only important to know that it is an essential component of the framework for our thought processes and, therefore, a significant factor in determining how resilient we will be. Once we understand this and know how mindset is created, we can more easily guide ourselves in the direction of building the traits of a joyful resilience mindset, and make shifts where needed to achieve that goal.

As an NLP (Neuro-linguistic programming) practitioner and trainer, I use many of the techniques in the NLP toolbox to help my clients in making mindset changes or shifts amazingly quickly. NLP is a set of hundreds of techniques developed by Dr. Richard Bandler and Dr. John Grinder, beginning in the 1970s. Bandler and Grinder took research and information from a number of fields, studying the foremost researchers and practitioners, and basically compiling what worked into a new field of research and study. NLP uses the connection between the brain, how we process and use language, and our senses to help us quickly change thinking and behavior. NLP has become commonly used in many different fields and areas of life to change behavior, improve performance and increase influence. The techniques are amazingly simple and effective. One example of an NLP technique that works amazingly well is reframing. Reframing can be used in many different ways and situations, but basically what it does is change our perception, and changing our perception changes the viewpoint from which we operate thus changing our subsequent thoughts and actions. Suppose we change the definition of how we are looking at a particular event from a "problem" to a "challenge." A problem is something we worry about, may feel defeated by, or often stressed over. A challenge on the other hand is something to be tackled and overcome that has the promise of reward or positive outcome. We are more motivated and activated by seeing something as a challenge than as a problem and that is simply a matter of the associations that language has in our brains. Another simple and commonly used NLP technique for quick mindset change is anchoring. The way anchoring works is it associates an internal response with an external or internal trigger and when this anchor association is set in place it allows the response to be re-accessed at will when desired. Visualization is another powerful NLP technique that many people use not even knowing it is an NLP technique. When you repeatedly visualize or imagine something, your brain experiences it in the same way as if you are actually doing it and patterns for this behavior are set in motion in your brain. If a basketball player repeatedly imagines themselves making a certain shot successfully, it has very much the same effect as practice and strengthens his or her actual performance when they go to make the sho tin real life on the court.

In recent years, the study of neuroscience has been clarifying, confirming, and verifying how and why many of the techniques of NLP work so effectively, as well as other areas of psychology, including positive psychology, energy psychology, and neuroscience. This is why I love having this tool to use when I work with clients to help them transform their minds and lives.

Previously, I have mentioned Holocaust survivors as examples of mindset and joyful resilience. My friend and colleague, Dr. Yvonne Kaye, reminded me of a strong example of this when she said, "The man who changed my life and attitude was Dr. Viktor Frankl who wrote his book. <u>Mans Search for Meaning</u>, in an Auschwitz concentration camp and in that environment said, *"People make conscious decisions on the way they feel."* Amazing!

To end this chapter, I want to tell you about a guest that I had on my radio show/podcast, *Soul Fire Wisdom*, and the very inspiring and poignant memoir she has written. She is Dr. Lise

Deguire. I was well into writing this book on joyful resilience when I got an email from Lise's assistant inquiring about being on the show and talking about her book: <u>Flashback Girl: Lessons on Resilience from a Burn Survivor</u>. I thought it would be a great fit, so I was excited and honored to have her as a guest. Lise's story is compelling, starting with a fire when she was just four years old that left her burned over sixty-five percent of her body. She is an inspiring writer who tells her story masterfully and she is definitely an expert on resilience, both from her own lived experience and her career choice as a licensed psychologist. I loved meeting Lise and interviewing her on the show, as she is such an inspirational example of joyful resilience. I will post a link to our interview at the end of the chapter, but I want to tell you what I saw and learned from Dr. Deguire's beautiful memoir.

When I first started reading and heard what Lise had experienced and lived through I thought it was horrific, how could I possibly ask this woman to be joyfully resilient? With all that she had to endure in pain and suffering, physical and emotional, how could I ask that she do more than survive, as she so remarkably has? Then I saw in the pages of her book, the joy that peeked out from every corner of her being, how she grasped life, how it became her lifeline, and eventually, became her ongoing mindset. It was music, singing with her father on the way to hospital, or listening to music from her hospital bed, when she could calm her mind no other way. It was curiosity, imagination, play, then eventually books, friends, and maybe some skilled help where she could find it, but from the beginning, from the depths of her devastation and despair, little Lise sought out and tried to connect with joy. Roaming the halls in her hospital gown, the little four-year-old found joy in new discoveries and expanding her world. She looked for joy to relieve the deep pain and suffering that her journey was, and she sought it out in every experience and person she encountered. Eventually, she found it, and it became the strength that buoyed her up through the unbelievable things she had to struggle through. It became and still is her mindset.

In her book, Lise ponders the reason why she, the person who was most damaged at such a young age, with many, many more challenges ahead, became the strongest and last surviving member of her family. I believe it came from connecting with whatever joy she could find, holding on tightly then growing it, like a gardener tending a beautiful garden, into the mindset that has created the blessed life she now lives. Not without challenges or memories of those hard times, but with the firm knowledge that she has overcome them and has a good life now. At the end of her book, describing her life and the time just before she started writing her memoir, Dr. Deguire says this:

"Look at what you have made. Look at everything you have built."
With these words, I felt released into the present. Relief filled my chest. The present was glimmering, shining with love and hope. The dark past, full of loss and despair seemed to slip away, like an alligator descending into a river at night. I could release the sadness of my mother's suicide, and everything my mother was, or wasn't, to me. My focus was fully on the day I was having, and the marvels of my life as it has turned out. I started this book. I felt released forever."

I strongly recommend reading Dr. Deguire's book. It is not a self-help or how-to book, but a memoir, her story, that gives an example of stunning resilience and in the process some lessons that can help us all in getting through the worst of times, starting with the resilience and joy a little girl found in the darkest of places.

Follow the link below to view my interview "Finding Resilience" with Dr. Lise Deguire:

https://youtu.be/KcMOTMaRtSo.

Chapter Thirteen

"Our greatest weakness lies in giving up. The most certain way to succeed is always to try just one more time."

– Thomas Edison

Resilience Practices, Routines & Activities

A practice in the sense that I am referring to here is a ritual, exercise, activity, or set of habits that you perform on a regular basis to maintain focus and achieve proficiency. It is said that practice makes perfect and if that is not true, at the very least it improves performance, in almost everything we do. This is certainly true of resilience and joyful resilience, and there are some practices that definitely instill the qualities that build the traits we have mentioned to strengthen our resilience. Some of these practices are mediation, mindfulness, yoga, reiki, qigong, tai chi, and many more mind/body disciplines. Here I am going to talk a little about mediation, mindfulness, yoga, and reiki and how they work as practices in our daily lives to make us more joyfully resilient. I will also discuss other routines and activities that, when included in our daily lives, also aid us to be more joyful and resilient. These are all suggestions and there are many practices and activities that can be helpful to you, depending on your preferences and what fits in with your lifestyle and schedule. These things actually help you to create a supportive lifestyle that in turn makes you more resilient.

Meditation

Meditation is a well-established and long-practiced form of relaxation that is practiced by many. It can create a deep state of tranquility, relaxation, and mental focus. It eliminates the stream of jumbled thoughts, loops, and scattered pieces of information that often lead to stress and anxiety. Practiced over time, it is known to lead to better mental clarity and enhanced physical and emotional well-being. There are many ways to practice meditation with different forms and depths of meditative practice, but it basically just takes a small amount of time and a tranquil, relaxing place where you can focus and clear away the clutter. The idea behind mediation is that it connects mind and body. Studies have shown mediation to have positive effects on the brain, such as increased awareness, concentration, better decision-making, and clarity. It actually thickens the pre-frontal cortex and strengthens higher-order thinking. These areas govern memory, learning, attention, and self-awareness.

Mindfulness

Mindfulness and meditation are sometimes confused, but they are not the same. While mindfulness can be mediative, it isn't always, and being mindful is not meditation. The practice of mindfulness does induce some of the same benefits in the brain and body that mediation does though; it can create a strong calming and relaxing response that reduces anxiety and stress. The purpose of mindfulness is to pay attention, without judgment, to our thoughts and sensations, to be able to return to the present moment and achieve the desired state of calm and relaxation when needed. In other words, it is a kind of alert system that catches us when we go off-course, veering into the past or future and brings us back to the present moment where all is okay, or at least we are dealing with what is actually happening now. With mindfulness, we can learn to control emotions and decrease or eliminate stress, anxiety, and depression. It can help us focus our attention and observe things in an objective way. Below is a simple three-step mindfulness exercise:

1. Stop and focus.
2. Become aware of your breath.
3. Expand your awareness outward starting with your senses.

Practiced daily, mindfulness has many mental, emotional, and physical benefits including stress reduction, better immune response, better mood, and increased resilience.

Yoga

Yoga is a mind and body practice that combines physical movements and postures, breathing techniques, and meditation or relaxation. There are a number of different types and methods of yoga, but the main purpose of all of them is to increase strength, calmness, awareness, and balance in the mind and body. It can have the added benefits of helping to increase flexibility, muscle strength, and body tone. If done two to five times a week, it can be very helpful to both physical and mental well-being. The blending of mind and body aims to create harmony, as well as awareness, strength and connectedness.

Reiki

As a reiki master and practitioner, I am frequently asked to explain how and why it works. Reiki is a practice that falls into the area of energy medicine and is a little harder to explain than the other practices above. It has been around for a very long time though and is found to be very beneficial. It is a practice with very specific traditions and rituals, but the underlying element is the flow of energy and keeping that flow clear by removing any blockages, which has very healing effects. It works in a similar way to acupuncture and acupressure. Removing blockages in the energy flow in and around the body enables relaxation, it can reduce pain and speed healing, as well as improve blood flow and reduce stress. The rituals and traditions around reiki are less important than understanding the principles of energy, flow, and how this affects our health and well-being. The reiki practitioner is not actually healing the client, but facilitating the healing processes within the client's own body or mind. Reiki practice gives a structure that the practitioner can learn and use with clients that also helps to focus the energy and prevent the healer from unintentionally taking on the energy of the client. It was established as a practice in the 1920s, by Dr. Mikao Usui, drawing its roots from Indian and Tibetan traditions of centuries earlier. The awareness and practice of using energy for healing was, of course, around long before it was structured into a practice. Although anyone can learn and practice reiki and other modalities of energy medicine, it does seem there are some people who naturally possess the ability to use this healing and awareness gift. There is a story from my childhood that I like to tell. I only vaguely remember it happening, but it has been retold to me by my mother. I had a strong connection to animals from when I was very small and had no real fear of them. My parents noticed this and my mom especially was a little fearful of this, as she was afraid I might either get hurt or get germs or diseases from approaching and touching them. When I was about two years old, I was sitting on our front porch watching the robins. My mom had told me many times not to approach or touch them. She was watching me sit quietly focused on one robin that was hopping about. She noticed that it was hopping because it had a broken leg. She could see that I wanted to approach the bird and help it, so she warned me not to. I sat, frustrated but very still, then the robin hopped right over to me and stood there right next to me. My mom warned again not to touch the bird and was just about to tell me to come into the house. The bird hopped onto my hand and just sat there looking at me. I couldn't help it: I reached down with my other hand and gently stroked its back. The little robin chirped once as if to say thank you and then flew off. I have no idea what happened to that bird or if it was okay. I like to think it was. My mom didn't say a thing, but both she and I were perplexed by what had happened. I was aware of feeling confused by this ability my whole life, not really knowing how to use it or how to protect my energy in the process. It was not until I learned reiki, as a practice, that I better understood it and how I could use it productively. There is still a lot of mystery around this field of study, but we are starting to understand it better.

Journaling

Journaling is a practice that helps people to express their thoughts and feelings, to examine, reflect on, and release anxieties related to them. It can be very cathartic. It often helps people with symptoms of anxiety or depression to control their symptoms and improve or balance their mood. It helps to put worries, fears, and problems into perspective. It can also help you to realize that you are capable of a broad range of feelings and not stuck in just one. It helps you to realize thoughts, triggers, and self-talk, to therefore better manage and eliminate them. It allows you to track your progress and have a record of how you have been feeling over a period of time. This makes it easier to look at the big picture, rather than focusing on the small details of everyday life. Like other practices, doing it on a regular and continuing basis is most effective. When done continuously, many people recognize big shifts in attitude and mindset. This is why I have included the companion journal with this book *Simple Soul Thoughts:*

Collecting Moments of Joy to help in forming the core mindset of joyfulness that serves as a reservoir and resource for your resilience when needed. You can incorporate positive practices into your journaling to help you make changes and form better habits. Think of journaling as writing letters to a dear loved one.

Exercise

In addition to the obvious benefits of keeping you physically fit and managing your weight, a regular exercise routine of any kind has some other important benefits to the well-being of your mind, body, and spirit. It turns out that when your body feels good, your mind functions better and you are also in a better mood. Physical activity releases endorphins in the brain and also relaxes muscles relieving stress and tension. For many people, exercise is their go-to stress reliever and it really works. Exercise not only improves strength and endurance, but it delivers oxygen and nutrients to the tissues and cells in our body and brain leading to better functioning and better health. It helps the cardiovascular system, heart, and lungs to function more efficiently, all of which gives us better resistance to illness and disease, more energy, and better overall health. It even helps us sleep better. Exercise improves blood flow to our brain, which increases and helps the growth and repair of new brain cells, and prevents their degeneration. It is really amazing what a little movement and activity can do for us. Contrary to some common stereotypes, working out can actually increase your IQ far more than playing online brain games.

Connecting with Nature

Many people will tell you that just being in nature and the outdoors makes them feel good. It seems to have a calming and destressing effect. People report feeling happier and more at ease if they are able to spend more time outdoors on a regular basis. There are a number of reasons for this. One is getting a boost of vitamin D from the natural sunlight. Being outdoors also helps our eyesight and breathing fresh air is good for the body and the brain. If you spend a little time outdoors each day it has also been noted to improve sleep which helps the immune system and almost all of our body and brain systems function more effectively. Part of connecting with nature is realizing we are part of nature and our oneness with nature. Here are some ways to become more aware of our connectedness:

1. Hike in wilderness areas
2. Mediate outside.
3. Choose a GAIA spot and spend some time there daily. A GAIA spot is a place where you can observe the Earth and her creations within the greater scope of things. GAIA stands for Global Astrometric Interferometer for Astrophysics. A forest hilltop might be a good GAIA for observing the earth, sky and earthly creatures.
4. Earthing – stand barefoot on the earth or lie on the grass and feel the Earth's heartbeat.
5. Dance outdoors without the limitations of an enclosed space.
6. Take a quiet walk and notice all your senses.
7. Stand outside in the dark and acclimate to the darkness

These are just a few ways of connecting with nature. Studies have shown that when people feel connected to nature, they are generally happier and feel more of a sense of purpose with greater feelings of calmness, joy, creativity, and focus.

Music

Most people enjoy listening to music of some kind. It turns out that it is quite good for us in body, mind, and spirit, as well. Personally, I start my day with music and never spend a day without it. It seems that music has more positive effects than most of us would have thought. I would describe it as having a little magic to it, but really it is pretty explainable and scientific. Neuroscience studies have shown that there is a definite connection between music and mood, as well as memory, intelligence, and cognitive functioning. It has also been shown that music is better at evoking memories than looking at an old photograph, which tells us why music is so powerful in eliciting positive emotions. The reason for these feel-good effects has to do with neurotransmitters and the release of pleasure-inducing substances in the brain, such as norepinephrine and melatonin. Here is a list of some great benefits music adds to our lives:

1. Makes us feel happy
2. Improves performance
3. Decreases stress
4. Decreases appetite
5. Improves sleep
6. Strengthens immune system

7. Can help with depression symptoms
8. Increases focus and mood while driving
9. Strengthens memory
10. Eases pain

The effects of frequency and vibration with regard to sound and music have also been studied and found to have immense benefits for healing, motivation, and general brain health. They have even found that frequency and vibration measured from voiceprints can be indicators of health and well-being. Apparently, there is more to music than just what we hear. We do know though that regardless of whether it is scientifically produced tones to help us sleep and calm us or just music we love to sing along with or dance to, it makes us happy and it adds great value to our lives.

Self-Care

Self-care routines and practices are vitally important to our well-being, yet it is one area that many people ignore entirely. Everyone needs to feel cared for, yet many of us spend a lot of time caring for others and no time caring for ourselves. Sometimes we put ourselves on the back burner and often we are expecting or waiting for someone else to care for us. The truth is, caring for yourself is very important for your sense of self-esteem and confidence. It can remind you and others that you are important. When you are well-cared-for, you feel better, more confident in your own value, and others see that too. Having a regular self-care routine has been proven to reduce stress, anxiety, and depression. It can also improve overall well-being, focus, cognitive function, energy, and sense of happiness. It is amazing what a little time and attention from oneself can do! You are certainly worth a little of you own attention and you deserve to be at the top of your own priority list!

Social Connection

If the pandemic has taught us anything it is certainly the importance of social connection. It seems there is nothing that can get us down and diminish our mood more quickly than isolation. We are social by nature and connecting with others is critical for our mental and physical well-being. Studies have shown that a feeling of closeness and connection to others strengthens our immune system and increases our longevity. It has even been proven that a lack of social contact can be more detrimental to our health than smoking, obesity, or heart disease. The better social support system we have, generally speaking, the happier and healthier we will be. This is especially true as we age.

Creativity

For me, creativity makes me happy, but that's not all there is to it. Having regular creative outlets has been shown to reduce stress, anxiety, and depression. It can improve focus and cognitive function. It is also effective in a therapeutic sense, as it can help in expressing and processing trauma, helping people to work through negative emotions and building a sense of accomplishment and self-confidence. It is a great tool for developing collaboration skills, problem-solving skills, and seeing things from a new perspective. Studies have shown that having a creative interest makes people feel more productive and in control. Creativity gives us a chance to try out ideas and new ways of thinking. These are definitely skills that build and strengthen resilience. Creativity is also one of the most joy-giving pursuits we can engage in, as seeing our ideas come to life builds a sense of achievement and accomplishment.

Learning

Regular and lifelong learning helps us to keep our brains healthy and functioning optimally. It develops the skills we need to improve, use resources, set and achieve goals. It gives us confidence. No wonder it is an important aspect of being resilient. New learning is part of the growth mindset we discussed in earlier chapters and having a growth mindset is essential for both resilience and joyfulness.

Spirituality

Spirituality is the sense, belief, or feeling that there is something greater than or beyond oneself and one's own existence. It is a belief in connectedness or connection to something. There are many forms of spirituality from affiliation with various religions to more worldly or universal belief systems. The benefits or importance of having some type of spiritual practice is that it often promotes desirable values, such as compassion, forgiveness, or altruism. It gives us a sense of community, a sense of purpose and meaning, structure, and resources for coping with difficulties.

Having a regular spiritual practice has been shown to improve our lives in the following ways:

1. Better health
2. Better mental well-being
3. Reduced stress
4. Greater feeling of positivity
5. A feeling of being supported

Gratitude

I am sure you have heard how powerful gratitude and "counting your blessings," so to speak, can be in changing your thoughts and, therefore, your life. It is absolutely true and having a daily gratitude practice is one of the surest ways to use the power of gratitude in your life.

There are many recommended ways to practice gratitude, all of which will add value to your life, as building this necessary, empowering tool and trait will bring you more resilience and joy.

Most of the practices center on expressing gratitude and this is surely both a helpful mindset tool and a magnificent gift that we can give to others. Some helpful ways of incorporating this into your daily life are:

1. Writing down the things you are grateful for each day.
2. Sending a thank you to people who help you, made you smile, or otherwise made positive contributions to your life.
3. Complimenting and showing appreciation for others.

Neuroscience has discovered recently though, that the most powerful gratitude boost we get is not from showing and expressing gratitude to others, but in receiving gratitude and/or experiencing the receiving of gratitude. In his well-known podcast, *The Huberman Lab*, https://youtu.be/KVjfFN89qvQ, Andrew Huberman talks about the neuroscience of gratitude and what distinguishes the most effective gratitude practices in "Episode #47- *The Science of Gratitude & How to Build a Gratitude Practice*." It turns out that gratitude received, remembered, or imagined releases more serotonin in our brains, and, thus, has a greater effect in strengthening both our resilience and our joyfulness. This does not mean that we shouldn't or need not express gratitude, after all, we do attract what we give out, but what it does mean is that strengthening our joy and resilience with an effective gratitude practice involves thinking about, writing down, recalling, and imagining instances where we were on the receiving end of gratitude. When I thought about this, it made a lot of sense. After all, I get an immense amount of joy from helping my clients, both when they express gratitude directly and when I can sense the appreciation that they feel in being empowered by the changes in their lives. It is a big part of why I do what I do. There are other examples, though, of how this works.

If you watched the movie, *Freedom Writers,* or read the book you will remember that the students in the book were very much stuck in a victim mentality due to the hardships and adversity of their lives. They had a hard time thinking outside of that paradigm. When their teacher had them study the Holocaust survivors and the people who had helped them survive their circumstances, they were able to experience the immense gratitude that those survivors felt, and thus, it changed the way they thought about their own circumstances, their outlook, and their feelings of both gratitude and their perception or viewpoint of the world. They received a huge brain boost by seeing and feeling the receiving end of gratitude in others. They then went on to both express and receive more gratitude in their own lives.

When I recall the lovely bouquet of roses that a client gave me as a thank you after our coaching sessions or the heart-felt card that a client sent me telling me how well they were doing, I am boosting my own serotonin levels and building the circuits or neural pathways to send and receive more gratitude, ultimately, building my joyful resilience. Thus, don't stop feeling and expressing gratitude, just add in receiving gratitude for a more powerful impact.

If you don't already have these practices or routines in your life, adding some of them will build your resilience traits and help you on your journey to becoming more joyfully resilient.

Chapter Fourteen

"No matter how bleak or menacing a situation may appear, it does not entirely own us. It can't take away our freedom to respond, our power to take action."

— Ryder Carroll

Resilience Exercises & Tools

While practices, routines, and activities help us to be more resilient, there are also some exercises we can do that will help us build our resilience traits and skillsets, plus there are some tools that help us to do this. I am going to talk about some of those here, explaining how and why they work. While we learn resilience and strengthen the traits associated with resilience through experience, it can also be learned outside of real-world experience by replicating circumstances that build the traits and skills that lead us to be more resilient and joyfully resilient.

Exercise One
Doors Closed/Doors Open
Instructions

Think about a time in your life where someone rejected you or you missed out on something important or when a big plan collapsed. These would be points in your life where a door closed.

What was the door that closed for you? Write it down here or just think about it for a few minutes.

Now think about what happened after; what doors opened after? Write it down here or think about it for a few minutes.

What would have never happened if the first door didn't close? Write down those experiences in the spaces below (write as many experiences as possible that come to mind) or spend some time thinking about them.

Now clarify – write these down below.

The door that closed on me was:

The new door that opened for me was:

Reflect upon your experiences and respond to the following questions:

What led to the door closing?

_____

_____

_____

_____

_____

What helped you open the new door?

_____

_____

_____

_____

_____

How long did it take you to realize that a new door was open?

_____

_____

_____

_____

_____

Was it easy or hard for you to realize that a new door was open?

_____

_____

_____

_____

_____

What prevented you from seeing the new open door?

_____

_____

_____

_____

_____

What can you do next time to recognize the new opportunity sooner?

_____

_____

_____

_____

_____

What were the effects of the door closing on you?

_____

_____

_____

_____

_____

How long did they last?

_____

_____

_____

_____

_____

Did the experience bring anything positive?

_____

_____

_____

_____

_____

Which character strengths did you use in this exercise?

_____

_____

_____

_____

_____

What does a closed door represent to you now?

_____

_____

_____

_____

_____

This exercise was taken from Seph Fontane Pennock's "Positive Psychology Toolkit," Positive Psychology.com.

Results:

A big part of resilience in life is adapting to change. In fact, the only thing in life that we can really be assured of is that things will change. Coming to this realization, and then seeing and dealing with it in the most optimistic and productive way is a primary resilience trait and skill. Learning to deal with endings is hard for people, especially if it is something good or something we have appreciated in our lives. However, nothing, even good things, lasts forever. Some examples of things that often change or end causing people to feel discomfort and even suffering are job loss, ending a relationship or marriage, moving to a new home, and the loss of a loved one or friend. All of these things leave us with a feeling of loss or missing something, however, another way to see these circumstances is as a door that has closed and a corresponding door that is opening.

If we take a step further, the end of one thing is always the beginning of something else.

We always have the option and choice to stay focused on that old thing that no longer exists or we can make the choice to move forward and focus on the new door that is opening.

The goal of this resilience exercise is to develop an awareness of the following:

1. The end of one thing is also the beginning of another
2. One thing ending can make room in our lives for something else
3. There is positive, or silver linings, even in those things that seem negative
4. Personal outlook or perspective to see what holds you back from being more optimistic

This exercise is great for seeing how a small shift in perspective can lead to a more optimistic overall outlook.

Exercise Two
How I Survived

This is an exercise I used at my first talk at the Symposium for Personal Development at the Harvard Faculty Club, September 2016. My talk was not on resilience, but on techniques and how combining difficult modalities could lead to quick change for clients. As part of my talk, I had the audience members do a little exercise that turned out to be very impactful. I only later realized its relevance to resilience.

Instructions:

Pair yourself with someone you don't know and tell them something you would currently like to do, but you are afraid to do.

Answer these questions:

1. What are you afraid would happen if you did it?
2. What is the worst that could happen?
3. What is the best that could happen?

Now, think of the worst thing that has happened in your life that you survived.

Answer these questions:

1. Why was it the worst thing that happened to you?
2. How did you survive it?
3. What good or positive things came from going through this

Now think about the thing that you would like to do, but are afraid to do.

Answer these questions:

1. Is it bigger or worse than the worst thing that you have previously survived?
2. If you survived that, can you overcome and survive whatever you encounter in doing this new thing you are afraid of?
3. What is stopping you?
4. Is your fear real or imagined?

Results:

Most of us are stronger and have more resilience skills than we realize, some of which have already been well developed by prior experience. We sometimes let our fears overwhelm us and do not realize that we are well-equipped to deal with and overcome adversity or reach a goal that we see as daunting. This exercise can make you aware of your strengths and help you overcome your fears by putting them and the magnitude of a problem or challenge into perspective by realizing if you have already gotten through much bigger adversities, certainly you can find a way through a new challenge as well. I was struck by how much emotion this brought up for participants during that original exercise at the Symposium for Personal Development and how much impact it seemed to have. I have since used it with clients and in group settings with similar results.

Exercise Three:
Smile and Breath
Instructions:

Clear your mind and concentrate. Now simply smile! Even if you need to force yourself to do so. Keep smiling!

Now, breathe in through your nose and out through your mouth.

Inhale slowly and deeply, filling your lungs completely.

Exhale just as slowly, emptying your lungs fully.

Now, repeat this process three times, taking time to experience it.

Results:

This exercise seems simple and will only take you a minute or two to complete, but don't underestimate its impact on helping you to be both more resilient and more joyful. It is very empowering. There are several important goals in the exercise. First, it establishes the strong connection between our actions and how we function in body, mind, and emotions. It makes us aware of what we have control over and how impactful that simple control can be. With a simple smile, you can change your mood, the way your body is feeling, and elicit a new or different response from those in the environment around you. With your breath, you can calm your body, reducing stress and anxiety. You can control your emotions with breath and you can even control the beat of your heart.

Both of these have not only effects in the moment, but long-term health benefits. Simply smiling releases chemicals in the brain that help us feel better and respond better. Done together, these two simple processes can give you so much control over yourself and the way you feel, which makes you better able to respond positively to whatever may come your way.

These types of exercises build our brain and the neural pathways that lead us to the traits and skillsets we need to face adversity head-on and bounce back stronger and more joyfully resilient. There are literally hundreds of different exercises that can be done in client/practitioner settings, in learning environments such as schools, or simply by people who want to develop better resilience traits and skillsets. It is not the same as going through those deeply impactful life experiences that are often our teachers of resilience, but it is a way of strengthening the muscles, so to speak, and being better prepared when life throws us those inevitable punches.

There are also some very effective tools that can be used in helping us to be more effectively resilient and joyfully resilient. All of these tools work in different ways to achieve similar results and may be more effective or appropriate depending on circumstances, goals, and the particular individual. There are additional modalities and combinations of modalities that work and are effective in some situations. I am going to talk a little about the tools and how they work specifically with regard to helping clients to build resilience and be more joyfully resilient.

Hypnosis or Hypnotherapy

Hypnosis is a process through which a client is guided or induced to a trance state that aids in focusing the mind, relaxing the conscious mind, and accessing the subconscious mind. It is a heightened state of awareness. It is also a state of increased suggestibility where we can be guided to clarify and work through problems or challenges quickly. Using hypnosis, a practitioner can guide the client to view stress or trauma-causing events in a different way and change their feelings and perspective about a situation to be able to let go, to move forward and past those traumas. It allows behavior modification that will make us stronger when similar stressors are encountered in the future. It can eliminate fears and limiting beliefs and allow us to move past them. As a hypnotherapist, I regularly see clients change when everything else they have tried has failed.

We have all experienced a hypnotic state as part of our daily life experiences. It is a natural state that we all slip in and out of regularly, without really realizing what is happening. We are entirely aware of what is happening but have transcended to a state of more direct connection to our subconscious mind. Hypnotherapy is different from hypnosis, in that, it involves agreeing to enter this trance state of heightened awareness for a purpose or goal beyond simple relaxation and is guided by a practitioner. The purpose or goal is to improve health and well-being, in accordance

with the client's goals, through guided suggestion and subsequent action. The client can make this

type of connection using self-hypnosis. Either way the client is always fully aware and completely in control of what is happening.

Hypnotherapy Works

Results for Effectiveness
Comparative Study by American Health Magazine
(2007)

Psychoanalysis
38% Recovery after 600 sessions

Behavior Therapy
72% Recovery after 22 sessions

Hypnotherapy
93% Recovery after 6 sessions

NLP (Neuro-linguistic Programming)

NLP and hypnosis are really closely related, but for NLP techniques to work the client does not need to be in a trance state. NLP is really a toolbox of techniques that uses the way our brain connects and processes things related to language, communication, and the senses. An NLP coach can help a client first to see how they are processing information that leads to thought patterns, that affect their view of the world and ultimately their actions. Then, using techniques that will align the way our brain processes language and stimuli, the practitioner helps the client to quickly make changes that aid in achieving their goals. It is used effectively in many areas of life, including therapy, counseling, coaching, sales, public speaking, advertising, and politics to mention a few. NLP can be used alone or as a tool while the client is in the trance state of hypnosis. Some NLP techniques are very effective and used frequently in changing mindset and behaviors:

1. Anchoring
2. Reframing
3. Meta-modeling
4. Dissociation
5. Rapport building
6. Belief change
7. Visualization

While there is a whole toolkit of techniques, these seven are especially helpful for mindset change and, therefore, are also helpful for creating the joyful resilience mindset and strengthening our resilience traits.

EFT (Emotional Freedom Technique)

Emotional freedom technique or EFT is a self-help and treatment modality used to neutralize or eliminate negative and limiting beliefs that do not serve us well. It can also be used for the elimination of pain and stress.

EFT is also sometimes referred to as meridian tapping or just tapping, as it uses the acupuncture meridian points and light pressure. Its origins are ancient, but modern applications were developed by Gary Craig in the 1990s, based on his study of the work of Roger Callahan in thought field therapy (TFT). This was one of the initial studies in what is now known as energy psychology. Gary Craig, who started EFT Universe (now owned and operated by Dawson Church) refined EFT into simple techniques and that refinement has continued through measurable testing and studies. In combination with other therapies, EFT has been found to be amazingly effective in yielding fast and lasting results.

As an energy healing technique, it works with the acupressure meridians in the body to quickly change the energy and restore flow. It has a structured set of tapping and chanting repetitions that work to access our parasympathetic system and neutralize negatives. It is great for reducing stress or feelings of fear and can result in changing emotions.

"The cause of all negative emotions is a disruption in the body's energy system."

- Gary Craig

"Emotional Freedom Technique, or EFT, breathes fresh air into the emotional therapy process by borrowing from the Chinese meridian system. While acupuncture, acupressure and the like have been primarily focused on physical ailments, EFT stands back from this ancient process and points it directly at emotional issues. These, in turn, often provide benefits for performance and physical issues. It is dramatically different from conventional therapy practices and that is why it often works where nothing else will."

- Gary Craig, EFT Founder

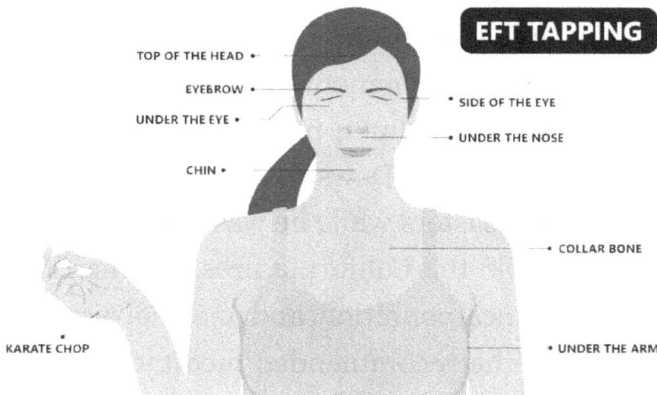

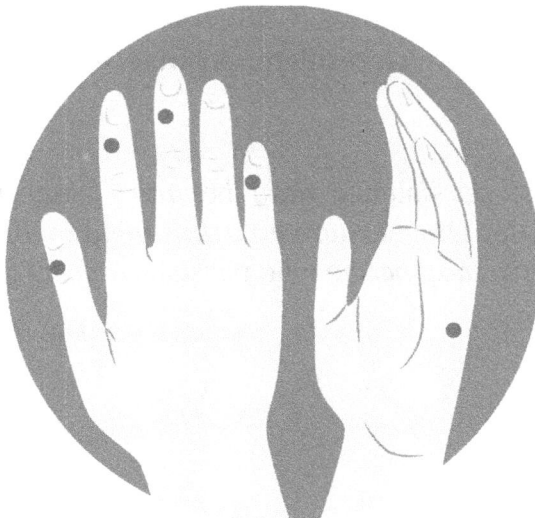

EFT TAPPING

TOP OF THE HEAD
EYEBROW
UNDER THE EYE
CHIN
SIDE OF THE EYE
UNDER THE NOSE
COLLAR BONE
KARATE CHOP
UNDER THE ARM

Dawson Church has expanded on this and taken the study of EFT further, making the connection between neuroscience and how EFT practice works with our brains. In his book *Bliss Brain: The Neuroscience of Remodeling Your Brain for Resilience, Creativity, and Joy,* he talks from his own experience and science about how you can rewire your brain through neuroplasticity. He explains how EFT can be used in this process and how quickly it can happen with the use of tools such as this. He provides a tapping and meditation practice where, in just twelve minutes a day, you can change your brain in eight weeks of daily practice. These changes become permanent or hard-wired new patterns in our brains that make us calmer, more resilient, and more joyful. It is extremely relevant that Dawson Church was experiencing his own life-changing disasters while he was delving into the science and writing his book: the California fires causing the loss of his home, a painful medical condition, and financial disaster. Through it all, he practiced the recommended meditation and EFT daily regime for achieving what he refers to as "bliss brain." He was his own case study in getting through those devasting hardships whilst still maintaining a resilient, positive, and hopeful outlook.

"The act of persistence may be more essential to the meditator than the permanent attainment of 'Bliss Brain.' The true hero may be she who persists, not she who wins."

– Dawson Church

CBT (Cognitive Behavioral Therapy)

CBT starts with the idea that our feelings, thoughts, physical sensations, and actions are all interconnected. From this it follows that negative thoughts and feelings can lead to undesirable behavior patterns and actually create a vicious cycle. In the process of CBT, these behaviors are broken down into smaller parts that can be better understood. It helps to recognize thinking patterns, then evaluate ways to change these with strategies for creating better ways of thinking and responding to the world around us.

Traditional Therapy & Counseling

This is sometimes called talk therapy, but can actually use many modalities. The main way of dealing with problems and issues though, involves the client talking about what they are concerned about and the therapist or counselor listening and helping to provide perspective and coping skills for the client to better understand and deal with life circumstances. It can be helpful because it is both cathartic and helps the client to believe they can change and improve their circumstances. It sometimes involves a diagnosis of a problem and depending on the circumstances and type of practitioner, it may involve medications or other interventions.

EMDR (Eye Movement Desensitization and Reprocessing)

This is a treatment used mostly in moving clients past trauma or post-traumatic stress disorder (PTSD). It is used by psychotherapists and counselors in a clinical setting and can be very effective. It is a guided therapy that concentrates on distracting the client from the impact of highly emotional events by using their own eye movements, redirecting them, and subsequently reducing the feelings triggered by those events.

Visualization & Manifesting

These are powerful tools and techniques that can be effectively used in many ways. Visualization is a well-established and studied tool (part of the NLP toolkit, but used in other areas as well) that can help to achieve and bring about desired results. There is a lot of science-based research and evidence on how visualization works and it is commonly used in many different fields to help us achieve the performance and outcomes that we want. According to the many research studies using brain imagery, visualization works because the neurons in the brain transmit information and interpret the imagery as the same or equivalent to real-life action. When we imagine a certain act, the brain sends an impulse that tells the neurons to "do" or perform the act or movement. As with most other things, the more you do it or the more it is practiced the stronger and more real it becomes. Here are some steps to making visualization effective:

1. Be very clear and specific about what you want

2. Have a visualization practice or mediation
3. Write it down
4. Create a map with steps to the goal
5. Take action

Visualization can also be more than just visual. You can use all of your senses and imagination in this process. You can feel it, hear it, taste it, really put yourself in the experience of it - whatever it is that you are creating. Personally, I remember using this technique as a child, before having any idea of what I was doing. And, not surprisingly, it worked. I have done vision boarding successfully many times and it is something I like to do on a periodic basis just to check in and see if I know where I want to go with my dreams and goals.

Manifesting is related to visualization and visualization is actually a tool or part of manifesting, but all manifesting is not visualization. Manifestation does not have the same scientific proof and validation behind it that visualization does. It is more of an emerging and evolving area of the energy psychology field. Put simply, manifesting means to bring something into being through thought, attraction, and belief. Through manifestation, you use the power of the subconscious to bring your desires to life. The idea is, if you think it, have intent, faith, and positivity, it will come to be. The "law of attraction" is based on manifesting. Scientifically, there is no concrete evidence to support the existence of the law of attraction and how it works, but there is evidence to support some of the components of it, such as visualization, positive thinking, and even to some extent, frequency vibration. Then there is intuition and how that works in our lives but is still something science can't put its finger on and quantify. There are many people who practice and believe that manifestation and the law of attraction are very real. It may be so, we just haven't connected all the dots yet. As a practitioner of many other modalities that worked before we knew why they did, I certainly would not be one to rule it out.

Life Coaching

Life coaching takes a slightly different outlook and approach than counseling or therapy traditionally has, although many counselors and therapists do use a lot of coaching techniques these days. One main difference is that there are no diagnoses in coaching. The coach starts with the premise that the client is capable of solving and working through their own issues and then goes about guiding them, giving them tools, resources, and coping techniques to help in reaching their desired goals. Coaching is appropriate for helping deal with many life problems and issues with everything from relationships, behavior change and stress but is not meant to tackle psychological disorders and dysfunction. Like therapists and counselors, coaches may use a variety of modalities, tools, and techniques in helping their clients depending on their particular training and background. This is always important to check out when selecting a coach or practitioner.

All of these tools can be helpful in developing our resilience and joyful resilience, those which work and be most effective will be individual for each client and their circumstances. Keep in mind that the main determinant of effective change, self-improvement, and empowerment is our desire to do so.

Chapter Fifteen

"The best thing about rock bottom is the rock part. You discover the solid bit of you. The bit that can't be broken down further. The thing that you might sentimentally call a soul. At our lowest we find the solid ground of our foundation. And we can build ourselves anew."

– Dr. Bindu Babu

Final Thoughts & Gifts

As I finish the final chapter of this book on joyful resilience, I want to tell you what is going on in my life and how I am feeling. I also have some gifts that I would like to share with you to help you on your own resilience journey. Some of the gifts are from me and some are from colleagues that are generously offering resources that they are passionate about and that will add to your resilience and joy. Although the journal that I refer to in the book is an optional companion to the book, using it in conjunction with and after reading the book will be a valuable tool for you in creating your most joyful and resilient self. I hope you will take advantage of the journal and the gifts, using them to your best advantage. When I thought of writing this book and first started writing it, I wanted it to be something that you would read and feel transformed to being instantly and automatically more resilient and joyful. As I wrote it, I realized that it had taken me years, if not decades, to go through this process and that it is still ongoing. I know it will be a process you too that will not happen instantly. I know the journey for each person will take different pathways and that we are never really finished. My hope is that I have made you aware of the difference between resilience and joyful resilience, as well as the added benefits that a core of joyfulness will add to your life, with some ideas and resources for creating that joyful resilience, and inspiration to get you started on your personal journey. I am hopeful that by reading this book you will achieve a state of joyful resilience with more ease and maybe more quickly than otherwise.

This has been a chaotic, turbulent and, to be honest, stress-filled time for all of us going through the pandemic with the political strife and division, numerous disasters of national and international magnitude, and then just dealing with the additional complications that all of this has caused in our individual daily lives. To further complicate things we were not exactly in a state of serenity before the pandemic hit and it will likely be a full two years, maybe three, before we put the pandemic behind us. I think I am actually being optimistic on that, so to say that this has been the time, at least in my lifetime, that has demanded the most resilience of us, may well be an understatement. I am not necessarily talking about resilience on an individual basis but on a collective basis. I can't think of a time when resilience has been more needed by so many.

It has taken its toll and I felt its effects like everyone else. Moving in the middle of the pandemic did add an extra element of stress to my circumstances. With so many restrictions and isolation, the move itself was more complicated, more costly, and took more time. I was also more on my own than I have ever been in my life and that made me more attuned to the isolation that we all experienced to some extent.

As a hypnotherapist, coach, and intuitive empath, I have been very aware of the stresses people have been going through and have also been very self-aware, checking in frequently on my own stress levels, as well as my mental and emotional well-being. After all, you can't drink from an empty cup or help others if you are depleted yourself. I have had to practice what I preach, so to speak, in getting through the difficulties of these times, and while writing this book this became very pertinent. The book has taken me longer to write than I expected. I expected to have it out in June 2021. Maybe that was too optimistic to begin with, however, it looks like it will launch a full six months late. I've been told that is not unusual for a book, but I personally know that some of the slowdown in the writing process was due to the extra care needed (a little bit of pampering and self-indulgence) I had to do along the way in reaction to the added stressors and the toll that they took. I found myself reaching a point of overwhelm from time to time, when my mind and body just said, "no."

It is now time to do a little celebrating, even though I'm not quite there yet in terms of having a finished book. I am going to turn up the music, dance around the house a bit, and maybe even sing. Oops! I forgot: I can't sing! The music and dancing are definitely happening though! Tomorrow, I am taking a mental health day as I've been putting my foot to pedal pretty hard the past two weeks since ending my weekly podcast, *Soul fire Wisdom*, and putting all my efforts into getting the book finished. I've encountered some glitches in the past several days: a power outage that resulted in some unsaved lost files that had to be reconstructed, computer problems, and a few days of not feeling great. Thankfully, things got back on track. There have been too few showers, days sitting at the keyboard for far too long in my sweats with no makeup and messy hair. Too many dinners of soup, salad or sandwiches, too late at night. I am feeling elated about getting to this point of handing everything over for editing and formatting in anticipation of seeing it become a real book. This truly is really exciting! I love all things creative, but I especially love seeing my creations come to life.

Tomorrow, I am taking a day off for a day trip to a small town on the other side of the beautiful Santa Rita Mountains, where I live in Southern Arizona. Every morning when I look out my window, the view takes my breath away! On the other side of those mountains, a little over two hours away, is a little town called Bisbee. I hear it is quaint and beautiful and has lots of little shops and art. Some say it is the prettiest town in Arizona and it is often compared to Sedona, which I love. I did my life coach training in Sedona and hope to visit there again soon too. On my trip I am going to take a leisurely drive over, visit the shops and take lots of photos, which I love doing. I will have a great lunch at the best little restaurant I can find. This is my reward for finishing the book, and I know it will help me get back into things to make sure everything that still needs to be done gets done, and that I finish publishing the book, so it's available for you to read!

I wanted to share this with you because I want you to know that I do the things that I have been telling you about in this book, that I believe in what I am telling you to do. I also want you to know that it works. When you feel doubts and think maybe it won't work for you, remember this – I was the woman who used to say, "If it wasn't for bad luck, I'd have no luck at all." I was the woman who reached a point of sleeping in her car, whose weight got over 200 pounds, who was sick for years and dwelled in financial chaos. I truly felt hopeless and not enough!

I started working for myself in 2007, I bought my first house on my own in 2011, and I became a life coach and hypnotherapist in 2015. I've traveled, attended seventeen concerts, and basically created a life I love. I bought my second house on my own in 2020, moving from Washington to Arizona. I continue to create a life that fills my soul, that inspires and nurtures my passions. I started really loving myself somewhere around 2005, and that love only grows as I evolve into the "me" I was always meant to be.

If I can do this, so can you, and I want you to know it is totally worth the effort. You are worth the effort!

Every day, I start my day first by making sure that I smile, even before I get out of bed, and then starting my day with a positive intention. I do my own version of mediation every morning to start things off and I use affirmations, visualization, and I have a couple of personal mantras I use. There is not a day that goes by that does not include music. I try to connect to the outdoors and get some time in the sun every day. I love walking and hiking and my ritual practice is reiki, though I am trying yoga right now too. I try to eat as healthily as possible, as I know that mind, body, and spirit are connected. I love learning new things, that is something I have always done and think I probably always will. I love creativity – art, writing, really anything creative – and I pursue these activities when I can. I am looking forward to traveling again (when we can) as that is a big passion for me. I try to pay attention to self-care and really take good care of myself, just like I would someone I love. Why am I telling you all this? I want you to know that I really believe in all of this, that it is all working for me, and that it will work for you too.

I am happy (no, not just happy), I am joyful most of the time and I do feel that whatever difficulties come, I am ready and I will find my way through them, not just surviving, but thriving, and feeling many moments of joy. I have a full reservoir to draw upon and I keep building it every day. I wish the same for you and I hope this book, the journal, and the other resources offered will be helpful for you on that journey.

Here are the gifts I promised. I am honored to gift them to you!

A Reiki Healing & Blessing Session

This is a personal audio/video gift from me that you can download and listen to or watch whenever you need it. It helps with healing and awakening mind, body, and spirit. You don't need to believe in or understand reiki for it to work for you. Just relax, enjoy, and heal!

Getting Started Journaling Video with Tip Sheet (PDF)

A gift from me to get your journaling started on the right track. If you haven't journaled before, this short video will help you make it work to your best advantage. I will give you some helpful tips and resources plus a few examples to get the ball rolling. Journaling can be one of the most effective tools for self-directed change.

Healing Music

An on-demand link by promo code to Music Quest Discovery video on demand. This is an audio and video instrumental soundtrack that uses much of the healing effects of music I have talked about in this book. Bill puts it this way: "Time-tested, safe and powerful, you will discover that music acts on us as much more than a quick fix and that a personalized listening practice can bring joy to you each and every time you need it."

From Bill Protzmann, founder of Musiccare.net, producer, musician, speaker, author, and 2014 award winner for the

National Council on Mental Wellness with an Award of Excellence – the industry equivalent of an Oscar.

Cosmic Love Meditation

A cosmic love meditation to connect you to the source of all unconditional-love-cosmic-oneness. This strengthens self-love, self-acceptance and helps you to be more grounded, elevates your vibration, and expands your state of mind, connecting you more deeply to your authentic self.

From Dr. Anna Margolina, Ph.D., founder of Outdoor Hypnotherapy, Ageless with Anna, hypnotherapist, coach, Tao energy healer, speaker, and author.

A Journey to Your Soul's Evolution

This meditation is for soul self-care, connection, and clarity. This is an area that Dr. Kelly has based her practice on and also practiced in her own life. She includes a healing bowl sound session, which I know you will enjoy as well.

A gift from Dr. Katherine T. Kelly, Ph.D., holistic health psychologist, founder of Soul Health Essentials, speaker, and author. She is working on the release of her third book, The Healer's Path, expected for February 2022.

Dealing with Grief & Loss – Best Tips & Meditation

This is a video with Dr. Yvonne Kaye giving the tips that she has found to work best in dealing with the process of getting through loss and grief and ending with a helpful guided meditation. Dr. Kaye has over forty years of experience to draw from and is a well-known expert in this area.

Dr. Yvonne Kaye is a thanatologist specializing in addiction and bereavement. She has over forty years of experience and has experienced grief and loss herself. She is an author, speaker, former radio host, and current podcast host.

For all of these gifts follow the link below to the book page on my **Soul Fire Wisdom Coaching and Hypnotherapy** website and then click on *Gifts* to go to the *Gift* page with more complete descriptions and links to these wonderful and very generous free gifts! Enjoy!

http://www.soulfirewisdom.com/Books/

You will also find links and information about the journal on the website:

http://www.soulfirewisdom.com/Books/

References & Notes

1. Webster, Miriam, *Webster's Unabridged Dictionary*, New York: Random House, 2005.

2. Tzu, Lao. *Tao The Ching*. Trans. John C. H. Wu. Boston: Shambella Press, 1990.

3. Salomao-Schmidt, Maria, *Finally Full of Yourself: Unlocking Your Spiritual DNA*, Boston, Happy Me Living, 2016.

4. Banyan, Calvin D., *The Secret Language of Feelings*, Tustin, CA, Banyan Hypnosis Center for Training & Services, Inc. 2003.

5. Hall, Steven M., *The Seven Tools of Healing*, Bloomington, IN, Balboa Press, 2018.

6. Sincero, Jen, You Are a Badass: How to Stop Doubting Your Greatness and Start Living an Awesome Life, Philadelphia, PA, Running Press, 2013.

7. Http://www.wikipedia.org

8. Hanson, Rick, PhD., Hanson, Forest, Resilient: How to Grow an Unshakable Core of Calm, Strength & Happiness, New York, Harmony House, 2020.

9. Graham, Linda, MFT, Bouncing Back: Rewiring Your Brain for Maximum Resilience and Well-Being, Novato, CA, New World Library, 2013.

10. Montminy, Zelana, Dr., 21 Days to Resilience: How to Transcend the Daily Grind, Deal with the Tough Stuff and Discover Your Strongest Self, San Francisco, CA, Harper One, 2016.

11. Hampton, Debbie, Beat Depression and Anxiety by Changing Your Brain: With Simple Practices That Will Improve Your Life, Scotts Valley, CA, Create Space Independent Publishing, 2015.

12. Brown, Brene, Daring Greatly: How the Courage to Be Vulnerable Transforms the Way WE Live, love, Parent and Lead, New York, Avery, 2012.

References & Notes

13. Bandler, Richard, Get the Life You Want: The Secrets to Quick and Lasting Life Change with Neuro-Linguistic Programming, Deerfield Beach, FL, Health Communication, Inc., 2020.

14. Deguire, Lise, Ph.D., Flashback Girl: Lessons on Resilience from a Burn Survivor, Philadelphia, PA, Dr. Lise Deguire, LLC, 2020.

15. https://newayscenter.com/change-your-thinking-change-your-life/

16. https://www.td.org/insights/the-growth-mindset-starts-in-the-brain

17. https://blog.mindvalley.com/which-part-of-the-brain-deals-with-thinking/

18. https://www.brainpickings.org/2014/01/29/carol-dweck-mindset/?utm_campaign=coschedule&utm_source=linkedin&utm_medium=Tina%20L.%20Huang

19. https://managementhelp.org/personaldevelopment/thinking/mindsets.htm

20. https://fs-blog-2021.mystagingwebsite.com/2015/03/carol-dweck-mindset/

21. https://thepeakperformancecenter.com/development-series/mental-conditioning/mindsets/

22. https://www.healthline.com/health/affects-of-joy

23. https://www.tandfonline.com/doi/full/10.1080/17439760.2019.1685571

24. https://www.blogtalkradio.com/think-believe/2021/03/07/shonte-javon-taylor-7-strategies-to-build-a-resilient-brain

25. https://drannacabeca.com/blogs/podcast/dr-sarah-mckay-neuroscience-health-hormones

26. https://www.heysigmund.com/brain-and-happiness/

References & Notes

27. https://drsarahmckay.com/six-brain-based-solutions-to-beat-stress/

28. https://www.linkedin.com/pulse/ten-life-lessons-resilience-debbie-hampton

29. https://elemental.medium.com/how-to-build-a-more-resilient-brain-5b00785868cc

30. https://laurenonlocation.com/changing-your-mindset/

31. https://www.inc.com/young-entrepreneur-council/12-ways-to-shift-your-mindset-and-embrace-change.html

32. https://thebestbrainpossible.com/writing-improves-brain-heal-emotions-health-journaling/

33. https://positivepsychology.com/resilience-quotes/

34. https://link.springer.com/chapter/10.1007/978-0-306-48544-2_2

35. https://developingchild.harvard.edu/science/key-concepts/resilience/

36. https://greatergood.berkeley.edu/article/item/five_science_backed_strategies_to_build_resilience

37. https://positivepsychology.com/teaching-resilience/

38. https://www.newyorker.com/science/maria-konnikova/the-secret-formula-for-resilience

39. https://positivepsychology.com/wp-content/uploads/3-Resilience-Exercises-Pack.pdf

40. https://elemental.medium.com/how-to-build-a-more-resilient-brain-5b00785868cc

41. https://www.geeknack.com/2021/04/10/7-best-nlp-techniques-to-change-your-life-and-realize-your-potential/

42. https://www.goodreads.com/en/book/show/51335096-bliss-brain

43. Church, Dawson, Bliss Brain: The Neuroscience of Remodeling Your Brain for *Resilience, Creativity, and Joy*, Carlsbad, CA, hay House, Inc., 2020

44. Bandler, Richard, How to Take Charge of Your Life: The User's Guide to NLP, New York, Harper Collins, 2014.

References & Notes

45. Anchor, Shawn, The Happiness Advantage: How a Positive Brain Fuels Success in Work and Life, New York, Currency Publishing, 2018

46. Bell, Jonny, Cognitive Behavior Therapy: CBT Essentials and Fundamentals, Kindle, 2014

47. https://psychcentral.com/blog/for-thanksgiving-week-4-quick-mindfulness-techniques

48. https://lauradifranco.medium.com/visualization-the-ultimate-how-to-guide-for-manifesting-in-2020-23cef67fcf45

49. Dwyer, Wayne, W., Change Your Thoughts, Change Your Life: Living the Wisdom of Tao, Carlsbad, CA, Hay House Inc., 2007.

50. Huberman, Andrew, "The Science of Gratitude & How to Build a Gratitude Practice," Huberman Lab Podcast, Nov. 2021. https://youtu.be/KVjfFN89qvQ

About the Author

Kate Olson believes strongly in creativity, self-expression and the role they play in living your optimal life. She believes in wholehearted living and the integration of mind, body, spirit wellness. Most of all, she believes in our uniqueness, our worthiness and our beauty. It is her mission to help clients see those qualities in themselves and to guide them on their journey finding path, purpose, and peace.

After taking a giant leap of faith, Kate spent the month of March 2015, in beautiful Sedona, AZ, getting her life coaching certifications, including hypnosis, NLP and reiki. She attended Bennett Stellar University and was amazed both by the personal transformation she experienced and by the value of the new tools she was able to add to her prior education, skills, and her intuitive and spiritual gifts. Now after practicing for six years, helping hundreds of clients, and evolving in her own life, she is certain that she made the right leap.

She is a **certified holistic life coach, an NLP master practitioner and practitioner trainer, master hypnotherapist, and reiki master**. She uses these skills individually and in combination, as part of her holistic coaching approach. Her website features a blog, where Kate regularly posts her own take on wellness-related topics and has invited other experts to share their views on topics of interest to her clients as well.

She earned her BA in psychology from Western Washington University, augmented with graduate coursework at the University of Washington in Counseling. After a career spent in sales and marketing, as well as owning several businesses, her experience brought her full circle, back to the work that first sparked her interest with a deep desire to contribute to the well-being of others. She has continued to expand her skills, to offer clients the best possible results. She obtained a second master hypnosis certification from Cascade Hypnosis Center with specialization in 5-PATH® and 7th Path Self-Hypnosis® methods and trained through EFT Universe to offer EFT (Emotional Freedom Technique) or tapping. She received additional training with Dr. Richard Bandler and John & Kathleen LaValle (Pure NLP) in NLP (neuro-linguistic programming) to be certified as a trainer offering specialized classes and Practitioner Certification Training. To be able to offer pain management and advanced stress management she received ICBCH certification in medical hypnosis.

As a "change adventure navigator," Kate inspires and guides clients to embrace change and its possibilities. She loves helping clients succeed when other methods have failed. She is a speaker, author, radio and podcast host, and a retreat and event facilitator, in addition to her private practice serving clients locally and online worldwide.

In her first radio show, *Embrace Change with Kate*, which began in October of 2017, she was overcoming her fear of public speaking interviewing guests who were also embracing change and encouraging her clients and followers to do the same. After two years, she changed focus with her second show, *Soul Fire Wisdom*, which is about pursuing your passions and the wisdom gained. Although that show recently ended, episodes are still posted and Kate is busy pursuing her passions and doing *Soul Talks*, which are conversations on pre-selected topics relevant to coaching, hypnotherapy, and many of the issues her clients face in their daily lives.

If you are motivated and ready to roll up your sleeves and work to make the big changes that will propel you toward the life you want, Kate can help you get there faster! Sign up for an no obligation **discovery session**. Email *soulfirewisdom@ gmail.com* or **call 520-225-9673.**

http://www.soulfirewisdom.com

http://joyfulkate.com

Praise for <u>Living in Joyful Resilience: A Roadmap for Navigating Life's Ups & Downs</u>

"Kate Olson has created a tool kit for learning how to find joie de vivre (exuberant enjoyment of life). Her experience in the personal development field is apparent in her guidance towards attaining and sustaining what she calls "joyful resilience". A recommended read for anyone ready to welcome more joy into their life.

> **-Anne Hunter Logue Author of "The Story of the Sun", "I Once Had a Tiger" and the upcoming book "Letters Out of Time".**

"Your guidepost for dodging life's curveballs. I enjoyed the beneficial messages interwoven throughout this book. It offers heart-centered daily suggestions to deal with any kind of adversity. Regardless of one's background, the ideas herein are worthwhile.

> **-Thomas E Ziemann, Motivational Speaker, Author, <u>Creating the Relationship of Your Dreams</u>.**

"Years ago, a friend and I came up with the idea that while happiness is just the icing, joy is the cake. What we meant by that is that happiness can be sweet, but fleeting and based on the 'ifs, like I'll be happy if/when'. Joy is the substance that needs no 'reason', and sustains us. This book feeds the reader with the delicious cake of joy that will help them become resilient thrivers. The stories in this book, both Kate's and the contributors, will inspire you to live joyful resilience full out!"

> **-Rev. Edie Weinstein, MSW, LSW, licensed social worker, psychotherapist, journalist, author, editor, interfaith minister, speaker, editor and PR Goddess.**

"Kate Olson did such a great job in presenting complex psychological ideas in a very reader-friendly format, which captivated my attention till the end. It is a delight to have this book as a resource for coaches and self-directed learners who believe that life can be both difficult and delightful, when JOYFUL RESILIENCE is added to the pool of knowledge and skills.

While I, as a scholar and educator, have been exploring the idea whether resilience can be taught, Kate Olson's chapters have already answered that question elegantly, effectively, and effortlessly. As a skillful and experienced Life Coach, Kate provides tips and resources that can help us in cultivating such traits as FLEXIBILITY, OPENNESS, and OPTIMISM."

-Dr. Larissa Chuprina, Positive Psychology Practitioner, ESL & Culture Coach, with professional interests in Cross-Cultural Adaptability, Self-Directed Learning.

"As someone who reads a lot of self-help books, I was surprised to find so many beautiful examples of how to apply a strategy that, to me, was fresh and compelling. New thought. I couldn't put it down. In, Living in Joyful Resilience: A Roadmap for Navigating Life's Ups & Downs, Kate Olson has knit the threads of science, philosophy, and critical thinking together to create a roadmap that leads us to a place of peace and hope in our daily lives. Her recommendation for infusing joy into the mix of our struggles, while we aim to become more resilient, could not be more timely. What's more, she does it in a way that is not at all condescending or pie in the sky. Rather, it is a wise and respectful invitation to step into our Higher Self."

-Kathleen "Kat" Ritter, Artist, Poet, Musician & Entrepreneur, she lives with her screenwriter husband, Mark Charles Ritter, in Washington state.